BE A CREATIVE CHANGEMAKER

A KIDS' Art Activity Book

BE A CREATIVE CHANGEMAKER

A KIDS' Art Activity Book

Inspired by the **AMAZING** life stories of **DIVERSE** artists from around the world

Paula Liz

Illustrated by Bambi Ramsey

ROCKPORT

Quarto.com

© 2024 Quarto Publishing Group USA Inc.
Text, Photos © 2024 Paula Liz
Illustrations © 2024 Bambi Ramsey

First published in 2024 by Rockport Publishers, an imprint of The Quarto Group, 100 Cummings Center, Suite 265-D, Beverly, MA 01915, USA.
T (978) 282-9590 F (978) 283-2742

All rights reserved. No part of this book may be reproduced in any form without written permission of the copyright owners. All images in this book have been reproduced with the knowledge and prior consent of the artists concerned, and no responsibility is accepted by producer, publisher, or printer for any infringement of copyright or otherwise, arising from the contents of this publication. Every effort has been made to ensure that credits accurately comply with information supplied. We apologize for any inaccuracies that may have occurred and will resolve inaccurate or missing information in a subsequent reprinting of the book.

Rockport Publishers titles are also available at discount for retail, wholesale, promotional, and bulk purchase. For details, contact the Special Sales Manager by email at specialsales@quarto.com or by mail at The Quarto Group, Attn: Special Sales Manager, 100 Cummings Center, Suite 265-D, Beverly, MA 01915, USA.

10 9 8 7 6 5 4 3 2 1

ISBN: 978-0-7603-7802-1

Digital edition published in 2024
eISBN: 978-0-7603-7803-8

Library of Congress Cataloging-in-Publication Data
Names: Liz, Paula, author. | Ramsey, Bambi, illustrator.
Title: Be a creative changemaker : a kids' art activity book : inspired by the amazing life stories of diverse artists from around the world / Paula Liz ; illustrated by Bambi Ramsey.
Description: Beverly, MA : Rockport Publishers, 2023. | Series: Creative changemakers | Includes index. | Audience: Ages 7 to 12
Identifiers: LCCN 2023020007 (print) | LCCN 2023020008 (ebook) | ISBN 9780760378021 (trade paperback) | ISBN 9780760378038 (ebook)
Subjects: LCSH: Art--Juvenile literature. | Artists--Biography--Juvenile literature. | Creative activities and seat work.
Classification: LCC N7440 .L59 2023 (print) | LCC N7440 (ebook) | DDC 700.92/2 [B]--dc23/eng/20230602
LC record available at https://lccn.loc.gov/2023020007
LC ebook record available at https://lccn.loc.gov/2023020008

Cover design: Tanya R Jacobson
Photography: Paula Liz
Illustration: Bambi Ramsey

Printed in China

To all the amazing artists who have inspired me. Especially my former and current students.

Contents

Introduction — 8

Thutmose (b. 14th c. BCE) — 11
Bust Sculpture

Gu Kaizhi (b. 344) — 17
Scroll Painting

Artemisia Gentileschi (b. 1593) — 21
Chiaroscuro Drawing

Anna Maria van Schurman (b. 1607) — 25
Drypoint Self-Portrait

Luisa Ignacia Roldán (b. 1652) — 31
Historical Figure Sculpture

Katsushika Hokusai (b. 1760) — 37
Changing Landscapes

Berthe Morisot (b. 1841) — 41
Impressionist Painting

Natalia Sergeevna Goncharova (b. 1881) — 45
Costume Design

Jamini Roy (b. 1887) — 51
Animal Motifs

Alma Thomas (b. 1891) — 55
Colors of the Cosmos

Barbara Hepworth (b. 1903) — 59
Subtractive Sculpture

Frida Kahlo (b. 1907) — 63
Symbolic Self-Portrait

Emily Kame Kngwarreye (b. 1910) — 67
Batik Painting

Arthur George Smith (b. 1917) — 71
Wearable Art

Jewad Selim (b. 1919)   **75**
Capturing Community

Lygia Clark (b. 1920)   **79**
Interactive Sculptures

Monir Shahroudy Farmanfarmaian (b. 1922)   **83**
Mirror Mosaic

Ladi Kwali (b. 1925)   **89**
Sgraffito Pottery

Kenojuak Ashevak (b. 1927)   **95**
Animal Prints

Rosemary Karuga (b. 1928)   **99**
Community Collage

Marisol Escobar (b. 1930)   **103**
Assemblage Portrait Sculpture

Margarita Azurdia (b. 1931)   **107**
Geometric Culture Collage

John Muafangejo (b. 1943)   **111**
Personal Narrative Prints

Pacita Abad (b. 1946)   **117**
Trapunto Quilt Painting

Bodys Isek Kingelez (b. 1948)   **121**
Utopian City

About the Author   **124**
About the Illustrator   **125**
Acknowledgments   **126**
References and Resources   **126**
Index   **127**

Introduction

CREATIVE CHANGEMAKERS

This book is a celebration of the lives and work of twenty-five amazing artists. These artists were leaders who imagined new possibilities through their work. Although they faced many challenges, they never gave up. Instead, they pushed creative boundaries, inspired others, and paved the way for artists like you!

The artists selected for this book come from different historical periods, regions, and cultural backgrounds. Together we will learn about their diverse experiences and grow our appreciation of artists worldwide. Some names might be familiar while others are new. To understand why we might not know all these artists, we need to look back at the history of art.

THE HISTORY OF ART

Art is a way to express and communicate our ideas. Before people could write, we used art to tell stories. Humans have been making art for a long time, and some of the oldest artworks are over seven hundred thousand years old!

Throughout history, there have been many famous artists. But most people only know the names of a few of them. That is because not everyone had the same access and opportunities. For a while, only people with money and power decided whose work was valuable and shown in museums. Even though the world is full of different cultures and people, these artists were often men from Europe. To better represent the global majority, this book features some amazing artists who have traditionally been left out of most kids' art history. Together we will learn about the remarkable things they did with their art!

HOW TO USE THIS BOOK

Inside are twenty-five biographies that tell the stories of different artists' lives. You will read about their childhoods and understand what inspired them to create. You don't have to read them in order—pick the ones that interest you the most!

There are also fun art activities to try. You will get to experiment with various materials, techniques, styles, and ideas these artists used. Some activities will be fun and easy while others will be challenging. Find what inspires you!

YOU ARE AN ARTIST!

When you make art, you are an artist! Like the people in this book, you have your own special way of creating. The activities throughout will give you lots of ideas. Although there are examples, try to avoid copying what you see. Instead, use them as inspiration for what you want to create! Remember, art is different for everyone and should be unique to you and what you like. This book is just the beginning of your creative journey.

NOW LET'S MAKE SOME ART!

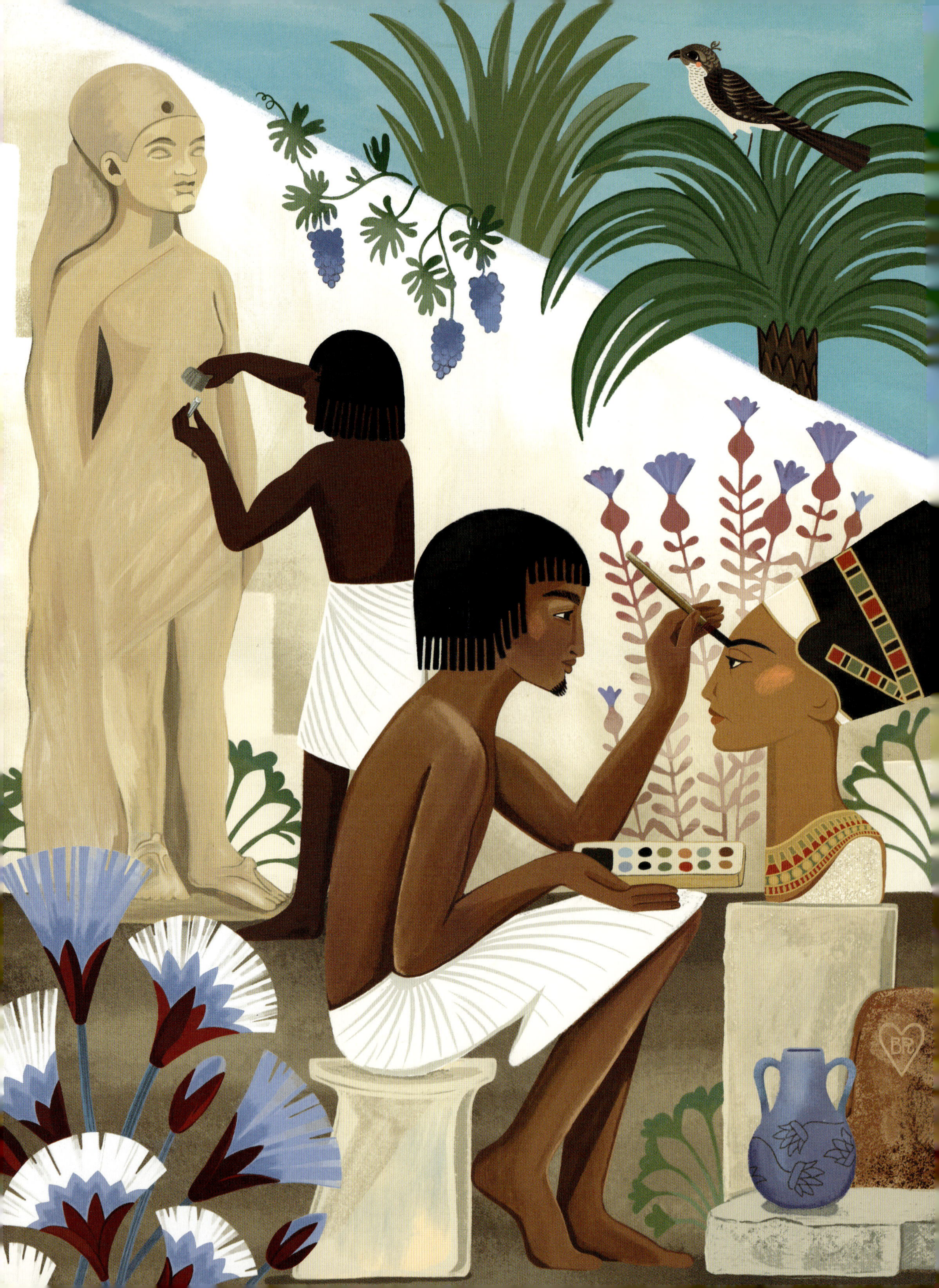

Thutmose

Date of Birth: fourteenth century BCE (approximate date)

Place of Birth: ancient Egypt

ANCIENT ARTIST

People have been making art for a long time. However, artists did not always sign their work. Because of that, we have yet to learn the names of many artists from the past. One of the few ancient artists we know the name of is Thutmose. He was an Egyptian artist who lived in a place called Amarna. Amarna is the name we use today, but it used to be called Akhetaten.

SUDDEN DEPARTURE

The king of Egypt, Pharaoh Akhenaten, hired Thutmose to make art for a new city he built in honor of a god named Aten. But after the Pharaoh died, the city was abandoned. Thutmose and others left to follow the new king, Pharaoh Tutankhamun. No one knows why Thutmose left so much of his beautiful art behind. Over time, people forgot about the city, and the earth covered Thutmose's workshop.

CHIEF OF WORKS AND SCULPTOR

A group of scientists who study past human culture, called archaeologists, uncovered Thutmose's workshop in 1912. They found writing in one of the courtyards that showed Thutmose was the chief of works and sculptor. Artists in ancient Egypt often worked with others on building sites such as royal homes and temples. Thutmose was the leader and would have managed other sculptors and artmakers in his workshop.

FAST FACT

His workshop remained undiscovered for over three thousand years.

ANCIENT DISCOVERY

The archaeologists found over fifty objects in a pantry inside Thutmose's workshop. Most of the items were sculptures of heads made of different materials such as quartzite, limestone, and plaster. One of the most exciting things they found was a sculpture of Nefertiti, the wife of Pharoah Akhenaten.

BUST OF NEFERTITI

The Bust of Nefertiti, Thutmose's most famous creation, was found in good condition considering it was over three thousand years old. Today, the sculpture is one of the most famous art pieces from ancient times. It's life-size and was carved from limestone and then painted with bright colors. Thutmose painted fancy patterns around Nefertiti's neck and put a crystal in one of her eyes. But the sculpture was unfinished, and it was probably just a model that Thutmose used to make other sculptures of Nefertiti. Even though it's not complete, it's still considered a beautiful piece of art, which is fitting because Nefertiti's name means "the beautiful one has come."

CONTROVERSY

The archaeologists took the Bust of Nefertiti and other things they found to a museum in Germany. But the Egyptian government claimed the archaeologists illegally stole the artifacts out of the country. Since the 1930s, they have asked Germany to return the sculpture to Egypt. As of 2023, the museum has yet to give it back. Unfortunately, this is common for many other ancient works of art. Changemakers worldwide have been working to return precious artworks to their original locations.

Bust Sculpture

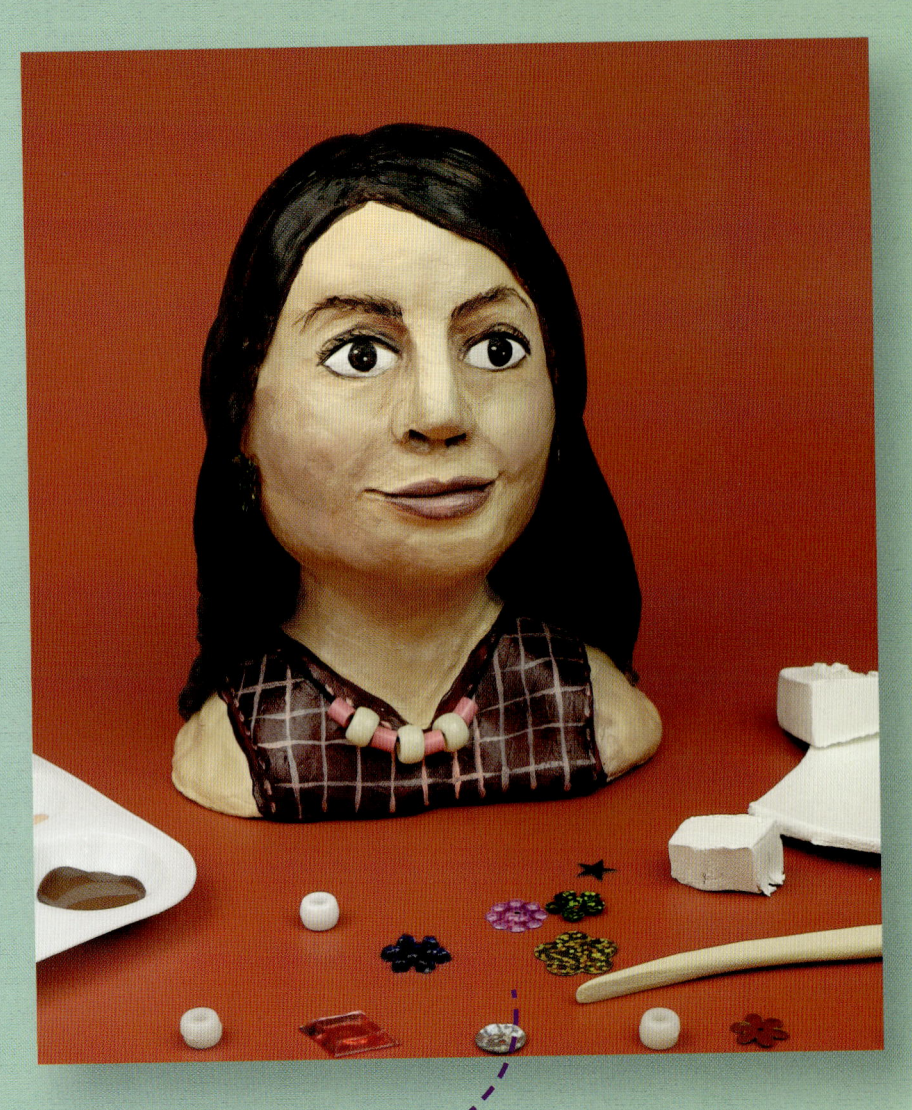

Sculpt a commemorative bust.

MATERIALS
- Cardboard 6" × 3" (15 × 7.5 cm)
- Hot glue gun
- Toilet paper roll
- Aluminum foil
- Masking tape
- Scissors
- Air-dry modeling clay
- Clay modeling tools (optional)
- Acrylic paint
- Paintbrushes
- Paint palette
- Water cup
- Mixed media, e.g., gems, pom poms, ribbons (optional)

ART CONNECTIONS

Ancient Egyptian artists like Thutmose made pictures of gods, pharaohs, and other important people. They would carve their faces into the walls of tombs and make statues out of stone to put in temples. Some portraits showed the whole person, from head to toe, while others only showed a bust. A **bust** is a sculpture of a person's head and shoulders. People have been making busts for a long time, and artists still make them today. Ancient Roman artists made busts out of marble to look like their family members while modern artists have made creative busts of people using materials like bronze and wood.

VOCABULARY

BUST: A sculpture of a person's head, shoulders, and upper chest.

COMMEMORATE: To celebrate or show respect for someone.

ARMATURE: A structure found inside a sculpture that provides support.

ADORNMENT: An accessory or item used as decoration.

12 BE A CREATIVE CHANGEMAKER: A KIDS' ART ACTIVITY BOOK

Let's Get Started!

1: Artists create work to **commemorate** those they admire. For this activity, you will sculpt a bust of a person important to you. Begin by thinking of someone who you want to celebrate. This person could be a family member, friend, or personal hero.

I created a sculpture of my mom, who taught me never to give up on my dreams.

2: Cut a piece of cardboard into a 6" × 3" (15 × 7.5 cm) rectangle. Use hot glue to attach a toilet paper roll to the center of the cardboard. This will serve as the base of your **armature**. An armature is found inside a sculpture and provides support. **Fig. 1**

3: Wrap the shoulders, head, and neck with aluminum foil to complete your armature. Use masking tape to hold any loose pieces together. Cut the cardboard base to align with the bottom of the shoulders. **Fig. 2**

4: Roll a piece of air-dry modeling clay into a slab and apply it over the figure. A slab is a flat piece of clay. Repeat until the entire bust is covered in clay. **Fig. 3**

(continued)

Fig. 1: Construct a base.

Fig. 2: Form an armature.

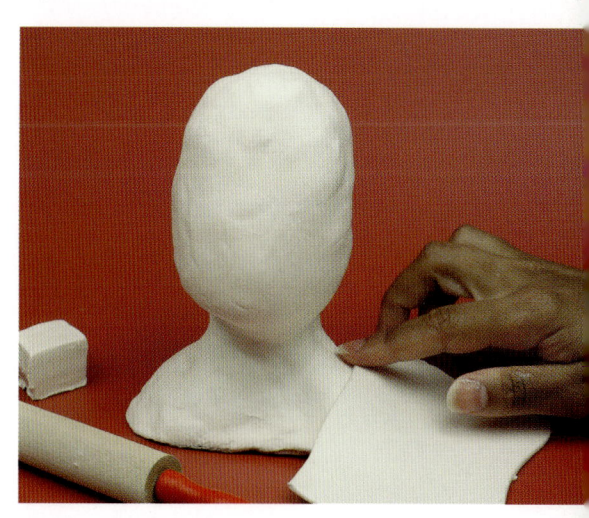

Fig. 3: Wrap the bust in air-dry modeling clay.

TECHNIQUES & TIPS

- There are many different types of clay. For this project, you want to use nonshrinking air-dry modeling or polymer clay. Most air-dry earth clays shrink when dried and will crack over the armature.

- If you do not have any clay tools, you can use a pencil or cutlery to carve details onto your sculpture.

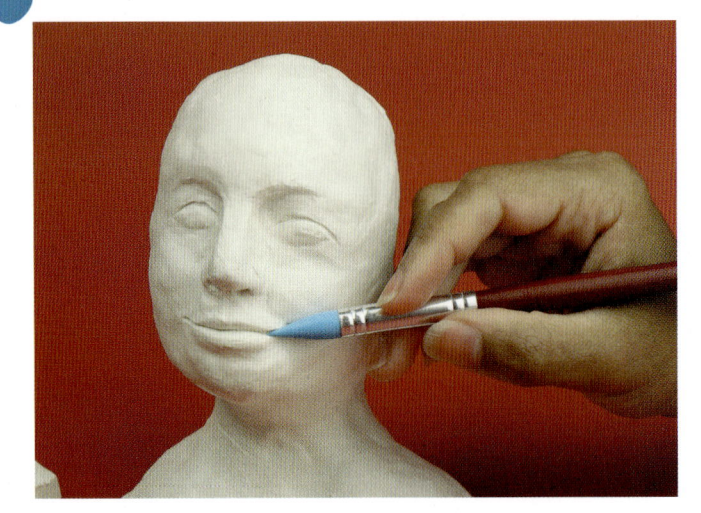

Fig. 4: Sculpt the facial features.

Fig. 5: Sculpt the details.

Fig. 6: Paint with acrylic.

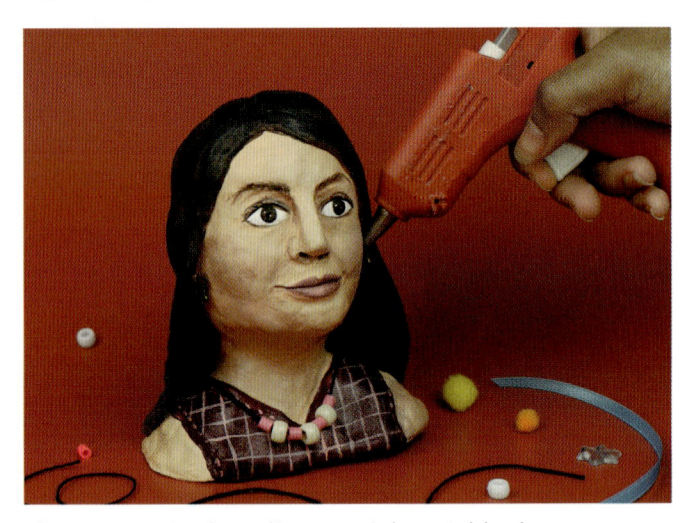

Fig. 7: Use mixed-media materials to add adornments.

5: Use your memory or find a photograph of the person you selected in step 1. You can look for pictures of them online or in a photo album. Try to find close images of their face from multiple angles.

Use tools or your hands to sculpt their nose, mouth, and other facial details. Be sure to look at your sculpture from all sides and compare it to any photographs you have of your subject. Don't worry about making it look exactly like them. Instead, try to capture their character and personality.

If you want more help sculpting the face, reference the sidebar on the following page. **Fig. 4**

6: Use clay modeling tools to sculpt their hair, clothing, jewelry, and other details. **Fig. 5**

7: Paint your figure using acrylic paints. **Fig. 6**

8: Some ancient Egyptian sculptures would incorporate jewels and other **adornments**. Adornments are accessories or items used as decoration. Feel free to include mixed-media materials to complete your bust. Some examples of mixed-media materials include beads, feathers, yarn, and buttons. **Fig. 7**

SCULPTING FACIAL FEATURES
Sculpting a face can be challenging! Here are some simple steps you can follow:

1: Using air-dry modeling clay, cut out the following shapes to use for your face:
- A large semicircle for the forehead
- Two small ovals for the eyes
- Two semicircles for the cheeks
- A long pyramid for the nose
- Two curved coils for the lips
- A semicircle for the chin

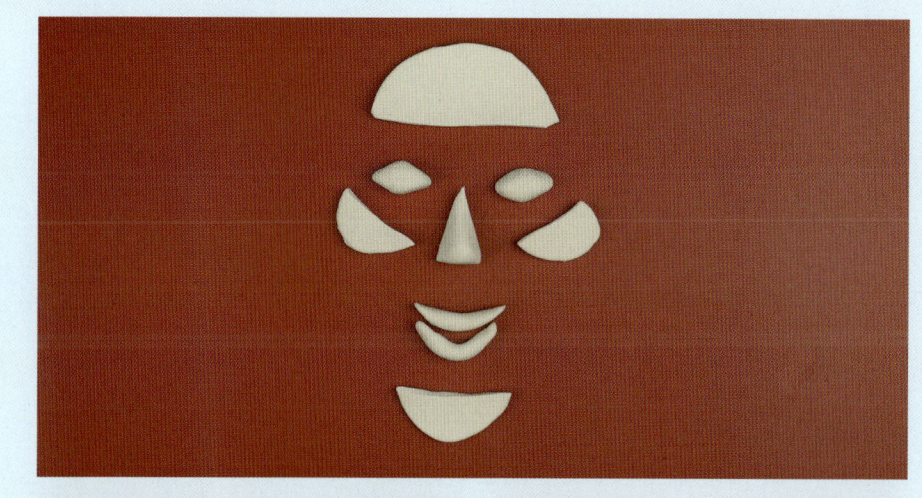

2: Cover your entire bust with air-dry modeling clay. Be sure to look at your sculpture from all angles while you work! The side view of a face is also called a profile.

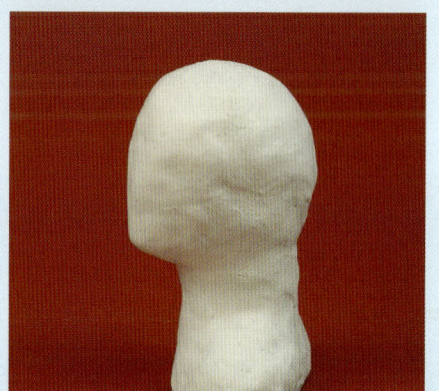

3: Attach the shapes you cut out in step 1 above onto the face.

4: Smooth the pieces onto the bust. Use clay tools or a pencil to refine the details.

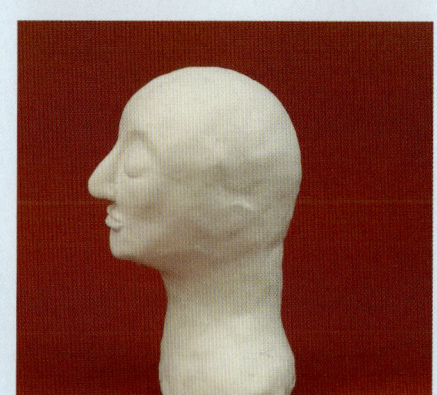

THUTMOSE

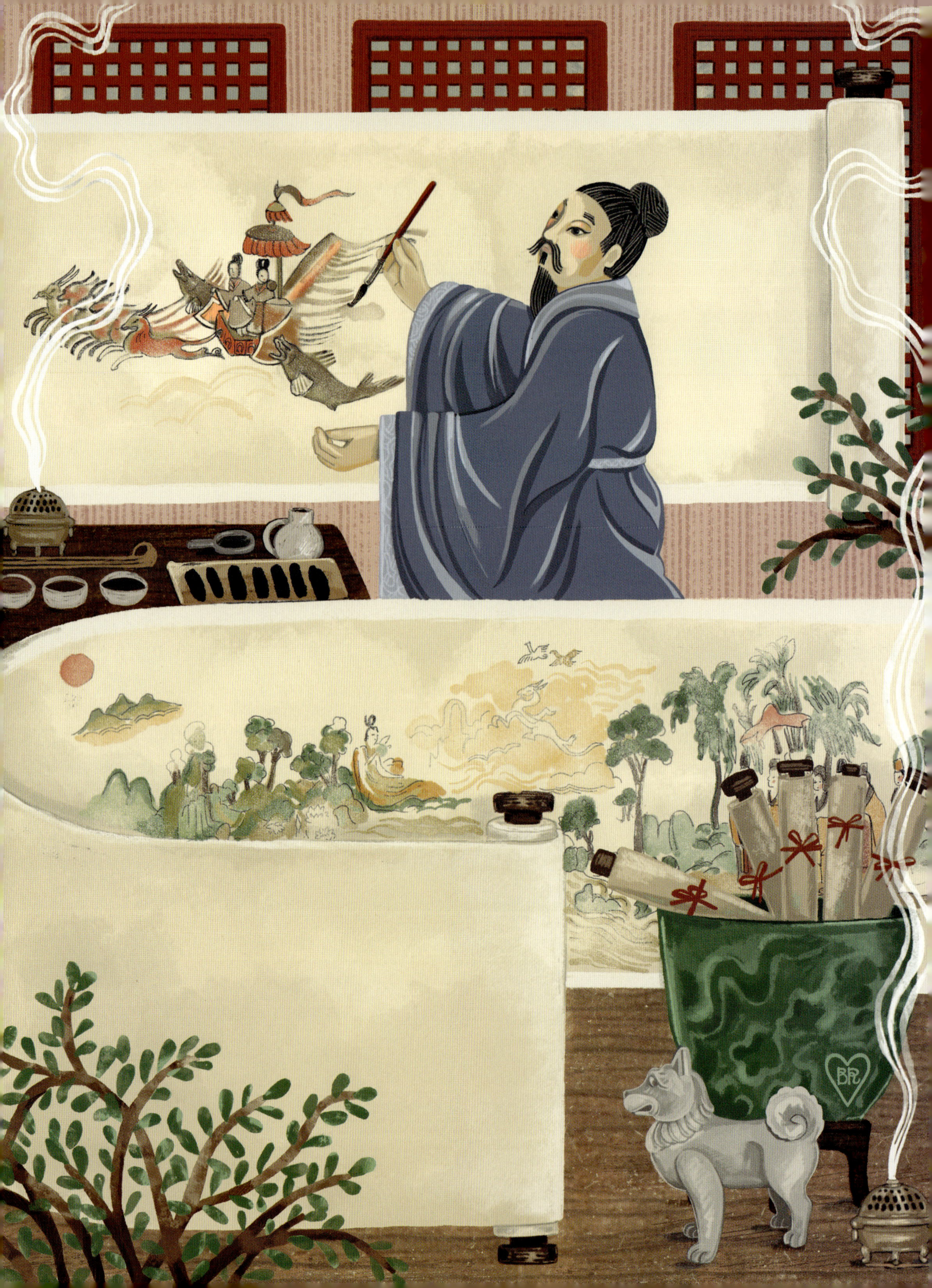

Gu Kaizhi

Date of Birth: 344 (approximate date)

Place of Birth: Wuxi, China

A MAN OF MANY TALENTS

Gu Kaizhi was born in Wuxi, China. He came from a bureaucratic family, meaning his father and relatives worked for the government. When he was younger, Gu Kaizhi was a royal officer to the emperor of China. But he had a lot of talents and is known as a poet, writer, and painter.

A LASTING LEGACY

Gu Kaizhi is considered the most famous painter of the Eastern Jin dynasty and a founder of traditional Chinese painting. He painted pictures and stories on long sheets of silk or paper attached to wooden rollers. These are also known as handscrolls. According to records, Gu Kaizhi created more than seventy handscrolls, but none of his original paintings still exist. Fortunately, we know about him because artists made copies of his handscrolls and wrote much about his art and life.

NYMPH OF THE LUO RIVER

One of those handscrolls is *Nymph of the Luo River*. This scroll illustrates a poem by the prince and poet Cao Zhi. It tells the love story of a prince and a nature goddess. The landscape is simple, and the two people are the main focus of the painting. As you unroll the handscroll from right to left, the story is revealed one scene at a time.

JOURNEY THROUGH TIME

Although the original *Nymph of the Luo River* is not around anymore, you can still see copies in museums in China and the US. These copies have a unique statement at the end called a colophon. Colophons provide information about the work and include marks from people who owned or studied it. This information helps show us the history of the painting and document its journey through time.

LOST IN THE PAST

We are still looking for more of Gu Kaizhi's original paintings. One story tells that Gu Kaizhi gave the emperor a box with his best paintings for safekeeping. But it is believed that the ruler took the art for himself, and Gu Kaizhi never saw them again. They might be hidden somewhere, lost, or even destroyed. Hopefully, someone may find them someday.

THE EYES ARE THE SPIRIT

Gu Kaizhi also wrote books about painting in addition to creating art. He noted that the most important thing in a picture of a person is their eyes because they show their true spirit. If you look closely at copies of his paintings, you can see a lot of detail and expressions in people's eyes.

FAST FACT
Only copies of his artwork exist today.

Scroll Painting

Paint a scroll that illustrates your favorite poem or story.

MATERIALS
- White drawing paper
- Scissors
- Pencil
- Pen
- Colored pencils
- Ink or watercolor paint, paintbrush, paint palette, and water cup
- Colored construction paper
- Glue stick
- Two wooden dowels
- Hot glue gun

ART CONNECTIONS

Artists in China have been making **handscrolls** since the fourth century. They would lay them on tables and unroll them from right to left to see the story. These scrolls differed from books because you could see the whole story in one long picture. Some artists, like Gu Kaizhi, painted poems on their scrolls while others painted wide **panoramic** landscapes. Later on, people started making vertical scrolls called *Kakejiku*. These scrolls stay unrolled and hang on walls as decoration.

VOCABULARY

HANDSCROLL: A long, horizontal scroll that unrolls and is viewed from right to left.

PANORAMIC: A full and wide view of an area.

KAKEJIKU: A vertical scroll meant to remain unrolled and hung on a wall as decoration.

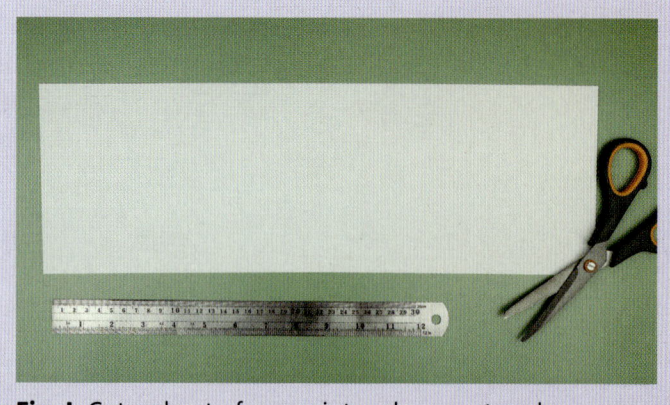

Fig. 1: Cut a sheet of paper into a long rectangle.

Fig. 2: Illustrate a poem or story.

Let's Get Started!

1: Before we begin, reread your favorite poem or story. If you can't think of one, write your own! You will illustrate this poem or story, so choose one that is meaningful to you.

The story I chose to illustrate is the Puerto Rican legend of the múcaro, a small night owl that lives on the island.

2: Scrolls were long and were meant to unroll when viewed. Start by cutting a sheet of white drawing paper into a 6" × 16" (15 × 40.5 cm) rectangle. **Fig. 1**

3: Using a pencil, illustrate your poem or story starting on the right side of your paper. Draw the various scenes and characters described in your story as you move toward the left of your paper. Use a pen to trace your pencil drawing. **Fig. 2**

4: Use colored pencils for the small details and add ink or watercolor to complete your illustration. **Fig. 3**

5: Cut a sheet of colored construction paper to 8" × 18" (20.5 × 45.5 cm) Glue your illustration to the center of the construction paper. **Fig. 4**

6: Wrap and hot-glue the wooden dowels around the ends of the scroll. Once the ink or paint has dried, roll your scroll and share your poem or story! **Fig. 5**

Fig. 3: Add color.

Fig. 4: Glue your illustration onto construction paper.

Fig. 5: Add wooden dowels and roll your scroll.

TECHNIQUES & TIPS

- Painting with watercolor and ink requires patience. Try using colored pencils for smaller details before you begin painting. Also, let the paint dry between layers or before adding another color. Otherwise, the different colors may blend into each other.
- If you don't have access to wood dowels for the handles of your scroll, you can use wooden skewers or disposable chopsticks.

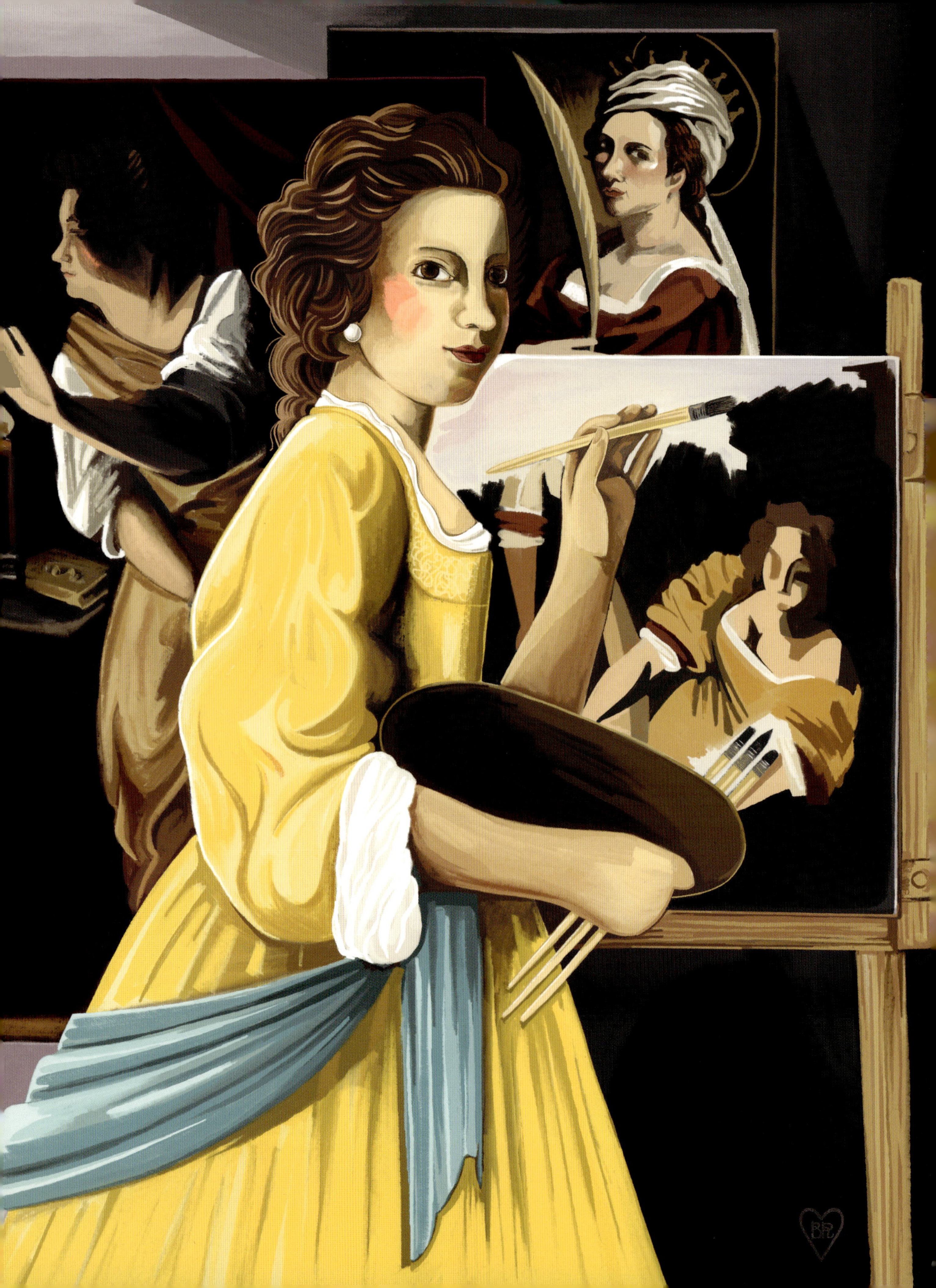

Artemisia Gentileschi

Date of Birth: 1593 (approximate date)

Place of Birth: Rome, present-day Italy

DAUGHTER OF AN ARTIST

Artemisia Gentileschi was born in Rome, Italy. She was the oldest child and the only daughter of the famous artist Orazio Gentileschi. When she was twelve, her mom passed away, and she had to take care of her little brothers.

YOUNG APPRENTICE

At that time in Italy, women did not have the same opportunities as men. It was hard for girls to become artists because they could not take art classes or buy painting supplies. Because girls had to be trained by family members, there were few women artists in Europe before the nineteenth century. But Artemisia was lucky because she learned from her dad in his art studio. Even then, it was hard for her to find models, so she often painted pictures of herself.

INCREDIBLE TALENT

Artemisia's dad knew she was very talented from a young age. When she was only seventeen, she completed her first signed painting. It was so good that some people did not believe she had painted it alone. A few years later, Artemisia became the first woman accepted into a special art school called the Academy of the Arts of Drawing.

BAROQUE ARTIST

Artemisia was an artist during a period called Baroque. Paintings during this time were dramatic, and the people looked like they were posing on a stage. The paint was very bright, and there was a lot of contrast and details. There was also a popular painting technique that Artemisia used called chiaroscuro. This technique uses light colors to highlight main figures against a dark background.

PORTRAITS AND ALLEGORIES

Artemisia painted many portraits of people and pictures that told stories called allegories. These stories illustrated important ideas such as love, life, and justice. Allegories were popular because they showed these ideas through images so even people who couldn't read could understand them.

TRAVELING ARTIST

In 1612, Artemisia married another Italian artist. They traveled a lot for work along with their five children. Important patrons like the Medici family and the king of England supported Artemisia and hired her to paint. She also made many connections during her travels and was friends with famous people such as the scientist Galileo.

SUCCESSFUL STUDIO

Later in her life, Artemisia settled in Naples and opened a very successful art studio. We don't know the exact date she died, but she was still living in Naples in 1654.

FAST FACT
She completed her first signed painting at seventeen.

Chiaroscuro Drawing

Draw a dramatic scene using chiaroscuro.

MATERIALS
- Black paper
- Colored pencils
- Chalk or oil pastels

VOCABULARY

CHIAROSCURO: The strong contrast between lights and shadows.

ALLEGORY: A symbolic story that represents a complex belief or idea.

CONTRAST: A strong difference between things.

VALUE: How light or dark a color is.

ART CONNECTIONS

Artemisia was a talented artist known for **chiaroscuro** painting. Chiaroscuro is the contrast between lights and shadows. The name comes from the Italian words *chiaro* (light) and *scuro* (dark). Artemisia would paint the people with bright colors and the background with dark colors. This contrast of colors makes the figures in the painting look like they are coming out of the picture. Artemisia was not the only one who used this technique. Artists such as Leonardo da Vinci and Caravaggio were also known for it. A similar contrast is sometimes used in movies to make a scene more exciting or dramatic.

Fig. 1: Draw the characters of the story.

Fig. 2: Draw the scene of the story.

22 BE A CREATIVE CHANGEMAKER: A KIDS' ART ACTIVITY BOOK

Let's Get Started!

1: Like many Baroque paintings, we can use an **allegory** for inspiration. Think of a story representing a belief or idea that is important to you. This story could be your favorite myth, fable, parable, or symbolic tale. Write a list of the important characters and events from the story.

2: Select one dramatic event from that story to illustrate. Use a white colored pencil on black paper to draw the characters. Consider what they are doing and how they are interacting with each other. Try to show emotions through their facial expressions.

I decided to draw a scene inspired by "Little Red Riding Hood," when the young girl encounters the wolf for the first time in the woods. For inspiration, I looked at the figures in one of Artemisia's paintings, *Corisca and the Satyr*. **Fig. 1**

3: Think about the setting of the event. Use a white colored pencil to draw the details in the background and complete the scene. **Fig. 2**

4: To re-create a chiaroscuro style, we must use a strong **contrast** of lights and shadows. Because the figures are often the focal point in a Baroque painting, use bright colored pencils or pastels for your main characters. Imagine a single spotlight and add different **values** to capture their three-dimensional forms. **Fig. 3**

5: To create contrast and emphasize the main characters, leave most of the background black. Use dark colored pencils and pastels to outline and highlight a few important elements. Like with many Baroque paintings, viewers may need to look closely at your work to see what is emerging from the darkness! **Fig. 4**

Fig. 3: Use bright colors for your main characters.

Fig. 4: Use dark colors for the background.

TECHNIQUES & TIPS

- Consider using a combination of colored pencils and pastels for your drawing. Use fine-tipped colored pencils for the small details and pastel sticks for the large areas.

- Artists use many types of pastels, the most common being chalk and oil pastels. Chalk pastels are soft and easy to blend with your finger but leave messy dust. Oil pastels glide smoothly onto paper, but their oily texture can be challenging to clean off.

ANNA MARIA A SCHVRMAN

Anna Maria van Schurman

Date of Birth: November 5, 1607

Place of Birth: Cologne, Germany

PROMINENT POLYMATH

Sometimes, people make art just for fun or to try new ideas. Anna Maria van Schurman was one of these people. She didn't make art full-time but still made a significant impact. Anna Maria was also interested in many things, such as studying religion, philosophy, plants, and medicine and playing musical instruments. She knew a lot about many subjects and was a brilliant polymath. A polymath is someone who knows a lot about many different things.

ACCESS TO EDUCATION

Anna Maria was born into a wealthy family in Germany and was lucky to have access to education. Even though girls couldn't attend school, she could still learn at home with her brothers. Anna Maria loved learning so much and could already read at age four. Later on, she studied at least fourteen different languages!

THE LATIN LANGUAGE

Anna Maria learned Latin, which her father initially only taught her older brothers. But one day, when her brothers couldn't answer a question, she quickly replied in Latin, and her father was very impressed. From then on, he included her in their Latin lessons. Latin was a language used mainly by men and was needed to go to university in Europe.

FIRST FEMALE STUDENT

Anna Maria wanted to keep learning more and attend school. At that time, women were not allowed to go to university. But she was so bright and knew Latin so well that she was accepted into the University of Utrecht. At twenty-nine, she became the first woman to attend university in Europe. Even though she was allowed to go, the school was worried she would be a distraction and made her sit behind a curtain during class. Despite this, she graduated with a law degree.

WOMEN'S ADVOCATE

After finishing college at the University of Utrecht, Anna Maria wrote about how girls should have the same chances as boys to learn and be educated. She believed girls were just as smart as boys and wrote many articles and books about it. One of her books called *The Learned Maid* was considered radical at the time because she said that girls should be able to be scholars too.

ARTISTIC TRAINING

Throughout her life, Anna Maria liked to teach young girls about all kinds of subjects, including art. She tried many different types of art, such as drawing, painting, cutting paper, embroidery, and printing. She learned from her mother and aunts and had a teacher named Magdalena van der Passe, who taught her more about engraving. She made an engraving of herself with a poem in Latin and sent it to other scholars. She made more art for her books, and in 1643 she became an honorary member of the painter's guild in Utrecht.

FAST FACT
She was the first female university student in Europe.

Drypoint Self-Portrait

Engrave and print a self-portrait.

MATERIALS

- 4" × 6" (10 × 15 cm) self-portrait photograph
- 4" × 6" (10 × 15 cm) sheet of plexiglass
- Transparent tape
- Scissors
- Metal stylus or etching needle
- Cardboard
- Printing ink
- Paper towels
- Printmaking paper
- Tray of water
- Towel

ART CONNECTIONS

Before the invention of the photocopier, **printmaking** was the only way to create multiple copies of artwork. Printmaking is when you transfer an image from one surface onto another. Artists cut, **engrave**, collage, paint, or stencil images onto a flat surface. The surface you put the picture on is called a printing plate. Printing plates are made of wood, metal, linoleum, or other materials. The artist spreads ink or paint onto the printing plate and applies it to a sheet of paper. The type of printmaking Anna Maria used is called **intaglio**. She would engrave marks into metal sheets and apply ink inside the cuts. Intaglio is different from another way of printmaking called relief printing. Relief printing is when you carve a picture into a flat surface and put ink on the raised parts.

VOCABULARY

PRINTMAKING: The art of transferring multiple images from one surface to another.

ENGRAVE: To carve or cut into a flat surface.

INTAGLIO: A printmaking technique where the artist carves an image into a flat surface and inserts ink into the indents to create a printed image.

Let's Get Started!

1: Anna Maria created several self-portrait prints that she would send to friends and family.

Begin by taking a digital photograph of yourself that you would like to share with others. Print a copy about 4" × 6" (10 × 15 cm) in size.

2: Tape your printed photograph onto the back of a plexiglass sheet. Cut any excess paper from around the edges. **Fig. 1**

3: With adult supervision, use a metal stylus or etching needle to trace your self-portrait onto the plexiglass. Remember to be careful when using sharp tools. Press down hard enough so you can see and feel the indents of your engraving.

When complete, remove your photograph from the plexiglass, creating a printing plate. **Fig. 2**

(continued)

Fig. 1: Print a self-portrait photograph and tape it to a plexiglass sheet.

Fig. 2: Engrave your self-portrait.

TECHNIQUES & TIPS

- If you don't have access to plexiglass, you can use recycled plastic instead. Search for a transparent plastic food container with a smooth surface. The top of clear produce containers works well. After cleaning the container, cut a small area for your printing plate.

- If you do not have a metal stylus or etching needle, you can use a long nail instead.

- If your printing plate moves around when you are printing, you can secure it to a table using tape.

- You may notice that drawing shadows in your self-portrait is difficult. Artists use hatching or scribbling to create value for materials that do not lend themselves to blending. By drawing short lines close to one another, artists can create the appearance of shadows. The more lines you draw, the darker the value. The fewer lines you draw, the lighter the value.

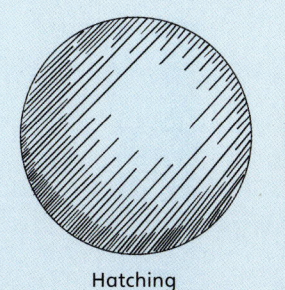

Hatching   Cross-hatching   Scribbling

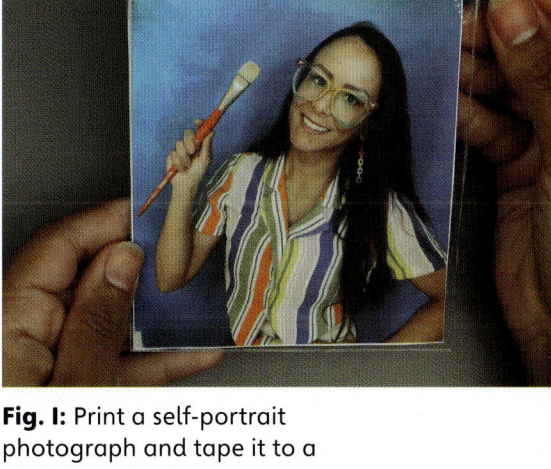

ANNA MARIA VAN SCHURMAN

Fig. 3: Apply and push ink into the indents of your engraving.

Fig. 4: Gently remove ink from the surface of the plexiglass.

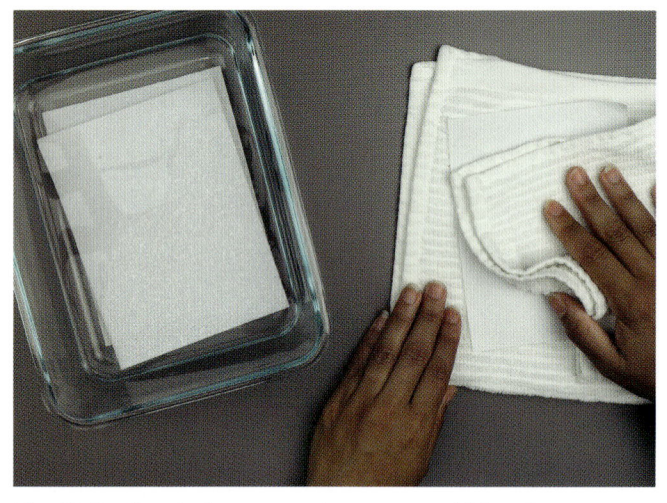

Fig. 5: Soak printing paper in water and blot dry.

Fig. 6: Place a damp sheet of paper onto your plexiglass. Rub the back of the paper to transfer the ink.

Fig. 7: Lift the corner of the paper from the plexiglass.

Fig. 8: Create more prints to share with family and friends!

4: Cut a piece of cardboard into a small 2" × 1" (5 × 2.5 cm) rectangle. Use the cardboard to add ink to your printing plate. Spread the ink across the surface, pushing it down into the indents of your engraving. **Fig. 3**

5: Crumple a paper towel into a ball to wipe off the excess ink. Move your hand in a circular motion to gently wipe away the ink on the surface. Make sure to use light pressure and leave ink inside the indents of your engraving. **Fig. 4**

6: Fill a tray with water and soak your printmaking paper for at least 5 minutes. Remove the paper from the water, place it onto a towel, and blot it dry. **Fig. 5**

7: Lay the damp paper on top of your printing plate. Make a fist with one hand and rub the back of the paper while using the other to hold the paper in place. Press firmly to make sure the ink transfers onto the paper. **Fig. 6**

8: Lift a corner to see how the image is transferring. Once transferred, you can remove the paper and place it somewhere to dry. **Fig. 7**

9: Repeat steps 4 through 8 to create another print. You can create as many self-portrait prints as you want to share with family and friends! **Fig. 8**

TAKE IT FURTHER!

1: Experiment using watercolor to paint your paper before printing.

2: Be sure to print while the watercolor paint is still wet.

3: Make a series of prints on painted paper.

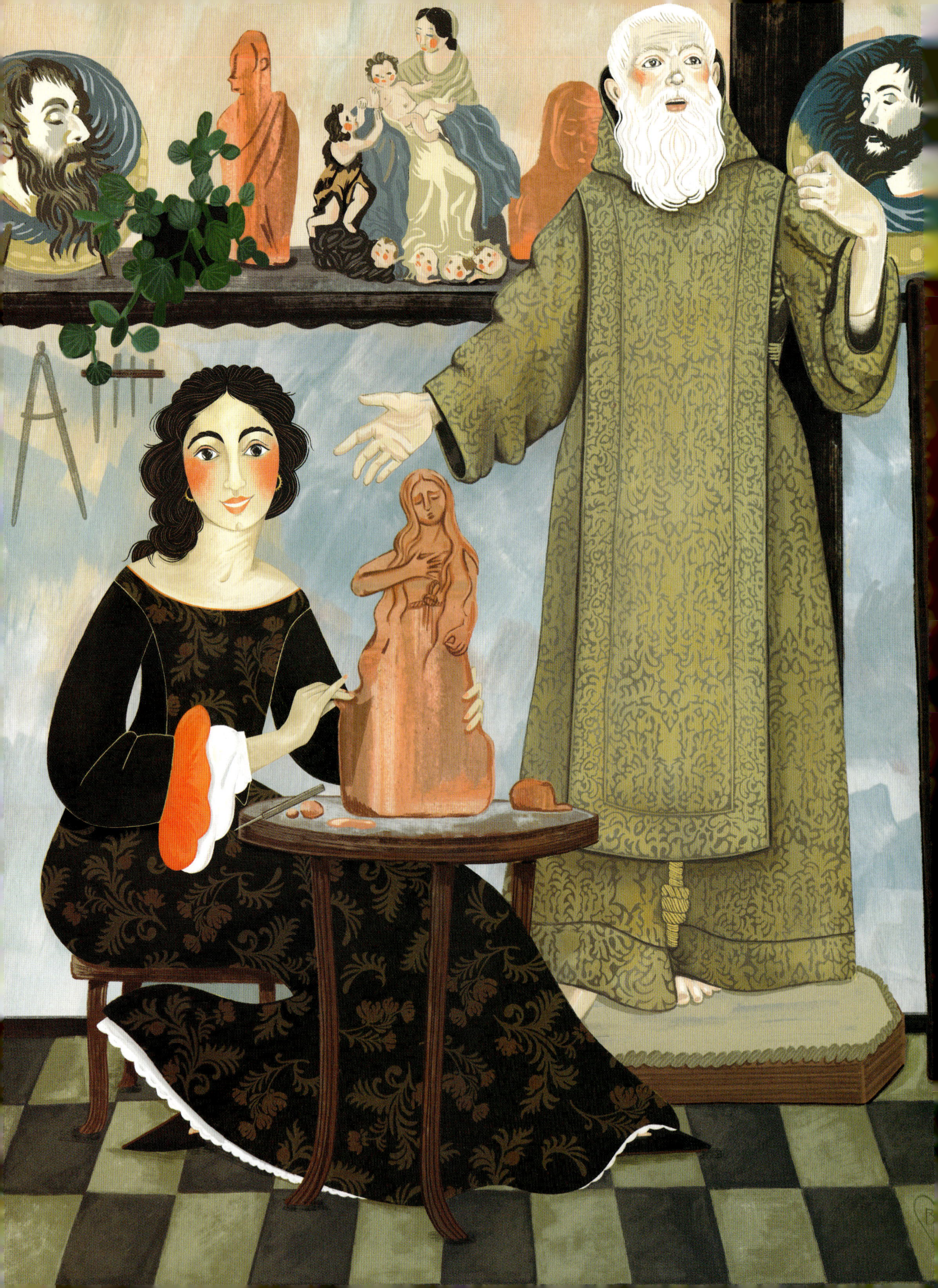

Luisa Ignacia Roldán

Date of Birth: September 8, 1652

Place of Birth: Seville, Spain

THE FAMILY BUSINESS

Luisa Ignacia Roldán was Spain's first recorded woman sculptor. She is also known as La Roldana. Her dad was a famous sculptor who taught her and her siblings how to make sculptures and paintings. They all made many works of art together in their workshop in Seville.

FORBIDDEN LOVE

When Luisa was nineteen, she fell in love with another artist at her dad's workshop. His name was Luis Antonio Navarro de los Arcos. They got married, but her dad disapproved and didn't attend the wedding. Because of this, Luisa left her dad's workshop and moved in with her husband's family.

INDEPENDENT ARTIST

Even though Luisa wasn't working with her dad anymore, she and her husband still made art. Luisa made the sculptures, and her husband painted them. At first, it was hard for them to find work. Not many people wanted to buy sculptures made by women, and people didn't respect their work as much as other artists'.

CADIZ COMMISSIONS

Instead of making whatever they wanted, many artists worked by commission. A commission is when someone hires an artist to complete work for them. Luisa got her first commission when she was thirty-two years old. After moving her family to Cádiz, the church hired her to make wooden sculptures for the city's cathedral. Later, the town council asked her to make wooden statues of the town's patron saints, St. Servandus and St. Germanus.

MOVE TO MADRID

After finishing her work in Cádiz, Luisa and her family moved to Madrid, the capital of Spain. In 1692 she applied for the position of court sculptor for King Charles II but was offered the role without pay. She said no but later accepted when the king promised to pay her a little bit and give her a home for her family. But at the time, Spain had money problems, and people had trouble finding food. Even though Luisa was an amazing sculptor, sometimes the king could not pay her, and the family had difficulty surviving. Just before she passed away in 1706, Luisa signed a declaration of poverty.

LASTING LEGACY

Even though she struggled, Luisa was an outstanding artist and blazed the trail for other women artists. After she passed away, she was given a special academic merit award by an academy in Rome. For years her style influenced the way other Spanish sculptors made their art. Today, you can see her sculptures in museums all around the world.

FAST FACT

She was the court sculptor for King Charles II in Spain.

Historical Figure Sculpture

Construct a sculpture of a historical figure.

MATERIALS

- 20" (51 cm) and 8" (20.5 cm) aluminum wire
- Scissors
- Aluminum foil
- Masking tape
- Hammer and nails
- Wooden block
- Plaster strips
- Water cup
- Air-dry modeling clay
- Clay tools
- Acrylic paint
- Paintbrushes
- Paint palette
- Water cup
- Permanent markers
- Mixed media, e.g., yarn, fabric, ribbon, hot glue (optional)

ART CONNECTIONS

Luisa sculpted multiple statues of famous historical and religious figures. Some were life-size and made of wood. She carved the faces to show emotion and included many details in the outfits. Luisa also made affordable tiny statues from clay. **Patrons** would collect her art and decorate homes, gardens, palaces, and chapels all over Spain. Patrons are people who buy and support an artist's work.

VOCABULARY

PATRON: A person who supports and purchases the work of an artist.

COMMISSION: When an individual or organization hires an artist to complete work for them.

BAROQUE: An art movement popular in Europe during the sixteenth and seventeenth centuries characterized by dramatic compositions, intense colors, strong contrasts, and many details.

Let's Get Started!

1: People **commission** artists to honor and celebrate important historical figures. Think of a person from the past you would like to recognize through a sculpture. Look online or in books to find a picture of them. If no images exist, you can use a description to draw them.

I decided to make my sculpture of Luisa Ignacia Roldán.

2: Create a wire armature for your sculpture of that person. Follow the directions below to help you.

(continued)

CREATING A WIRE ARMATURE
Follow these simple steps to make your wire armature!

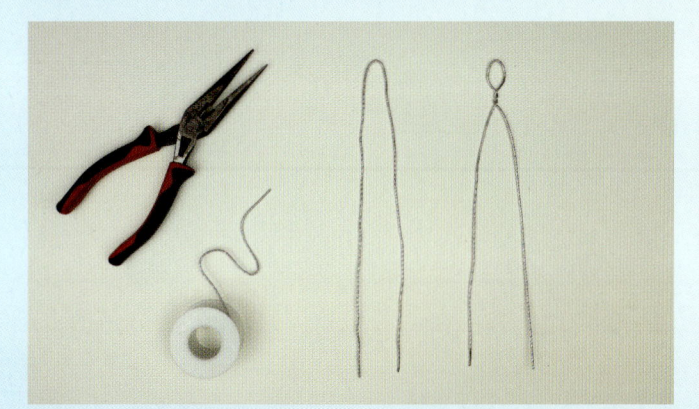

Fig. 1: Bend the wire in half and twist the top to create a small loop for the head.

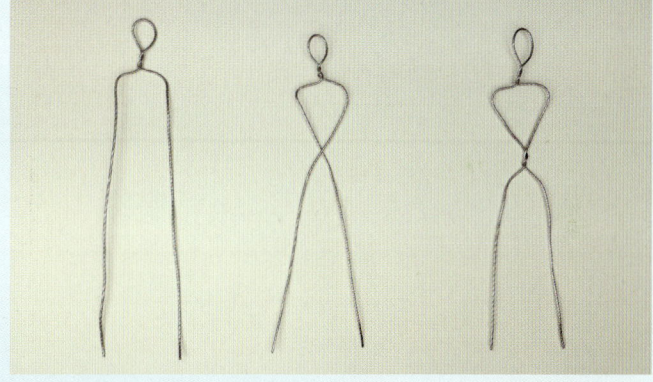

Fig. 2: Twist the wire to create a large loop for the body, pulling the ends apart for the legs.

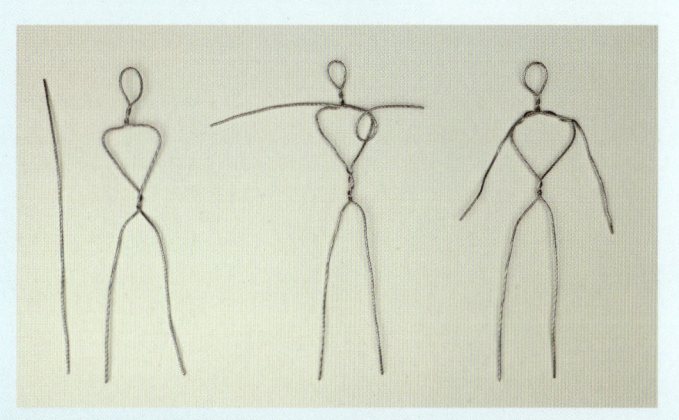

Fig. 3: Place the shorter wire through the body and twist it around the large loop to create arms.

1: Cut a 20" (51 cm) piece of wire. Bend it in half and twist the top to create a small loop for the head. **Fig. 1**

2: Separate the wire to create shoulders. Create a large loop for the body and twist the wire together. Pull the wire apart for the legs. **Fig. 2**

3: Cut an 8" (20.5 cm) piece of wire for the arms. Place it through the center of the large loop. Twist the short wire around the long wire at the top-right to create an arm. Twist it again on the top-left to create the other arm. **Fig. 3**

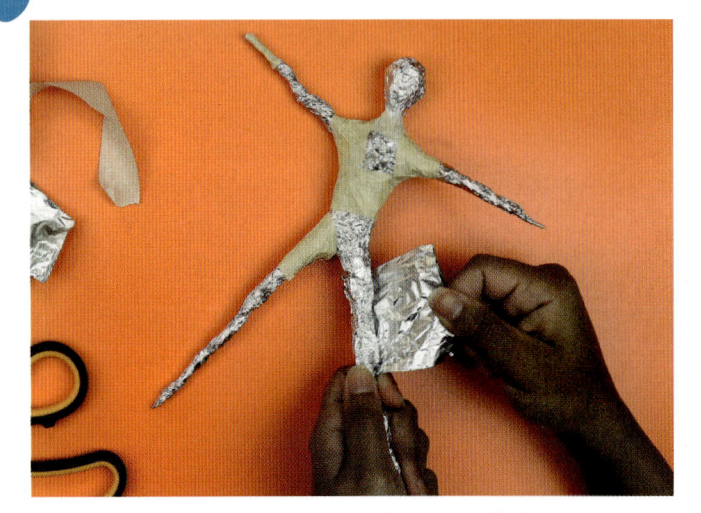

Fig. 4: Wrap your armature in aluminum foil.

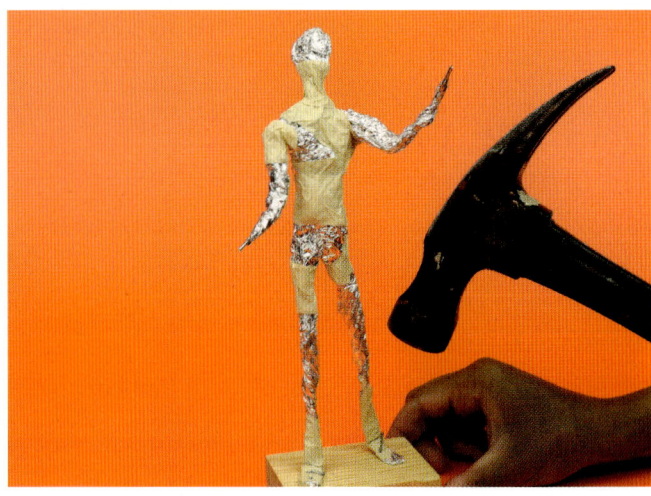

Fig. 5: Pose and attach your figure sculpture to a wood base.

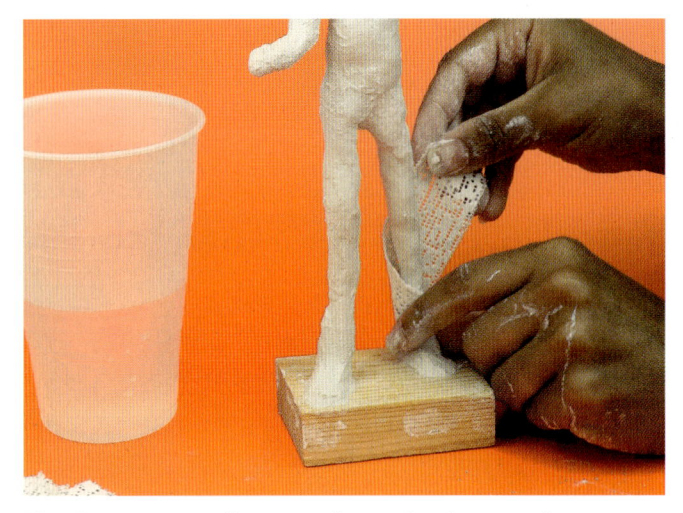

Fig. 6: Wrap your figure sculpture in plaster strips.

Fig. 7: Use air-dry modeling clay to sculpt the face.

Fig. 8: Sculpt the hair, clothes, and other details.

Fig. 9: Paint your figure sculpture and base.

3: Wrap your armature in aluminum foil to make a three-dimensional body. Be sure to look at your sculpture from all sides and use masking tape to secure the aluminum foil. **Fig. 4**

4: Use a hammer and small nails to firmly attach the feet of your sculpture onto a wooden base. Pose your figure before moving on to the next step. **Fig. 5**

5: Cut plaster strips into 2" (5 cm) pieces. Dip the strips in water before applying them to your sculpture. Repeat until you have covered the entire figure in plaster. **Fig. 6**

6: Reference your image from step 1. Use air-dry modeling clay to sculpt facial features and details. **Fig. 7**

7: Use air-dry modeling clay to sculpt hair, clothes, and other details. Use clay tools to add texture to the hair. **Fig. 8**

8: Once your sculpture has dried, use acrylics to paint your figure sculpture and base. **Fig. 9**

9: You can use paint or permanent markers to add small details like eyes, brows, and a mouth. **Fig. 10**

10: Use mixed-media materials to add details and complete your figure sculpture.

Think about how you can honor the person you are making a sculpture of through the objects they are holding and the clothes they are wearing.

Since Luisa Ignacia Roldán was known for her wood sculptures, I added a chisel and hammer to her hands. **Fig. 11**

Fig. 10: Use paint or permanent markers to add small details.

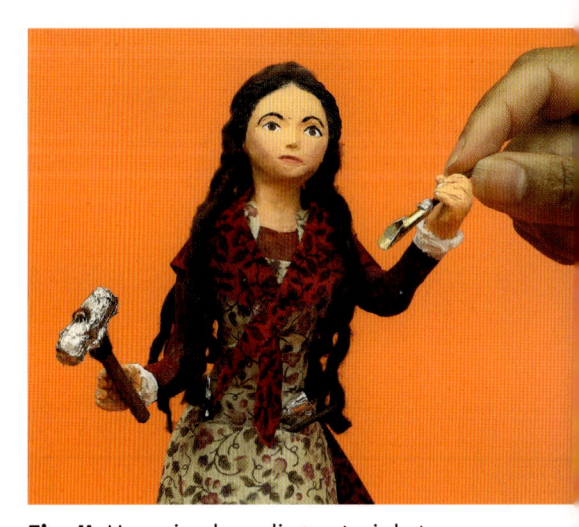

Fig. 11: Use mixed-media materials to add details and complete your figure sculpture.

TECHNIQUES & TIP

- Plaster can be fun but messy! Place newspaper on the table before you start working. It is easier to cut all your plaster pieces before you begin to add water. For this activity, I used about thirty 2" (5 cm) strips. As you apply the plaster to your sculpture, dip only one piece into the water at a time. When the water touches the plaster, the plaster starts to harden. Attach each strip securely to your sculpture and smooth the surface before adding another strip.

- **Baroque** artists such as Luisa would position the figures in their work in dramatic and expressive ways. Think about how you can pose your figure in an exciting way that shows movement and tells a story.

- Get creative with the mixed-media elements! Feel free to use yarn or felt for the hair and scraps of fabric for the clothes. In addition to their likeness, consider what objects you may add to your historical figure. Think about how you can celebrate their importance and honor their legacy.

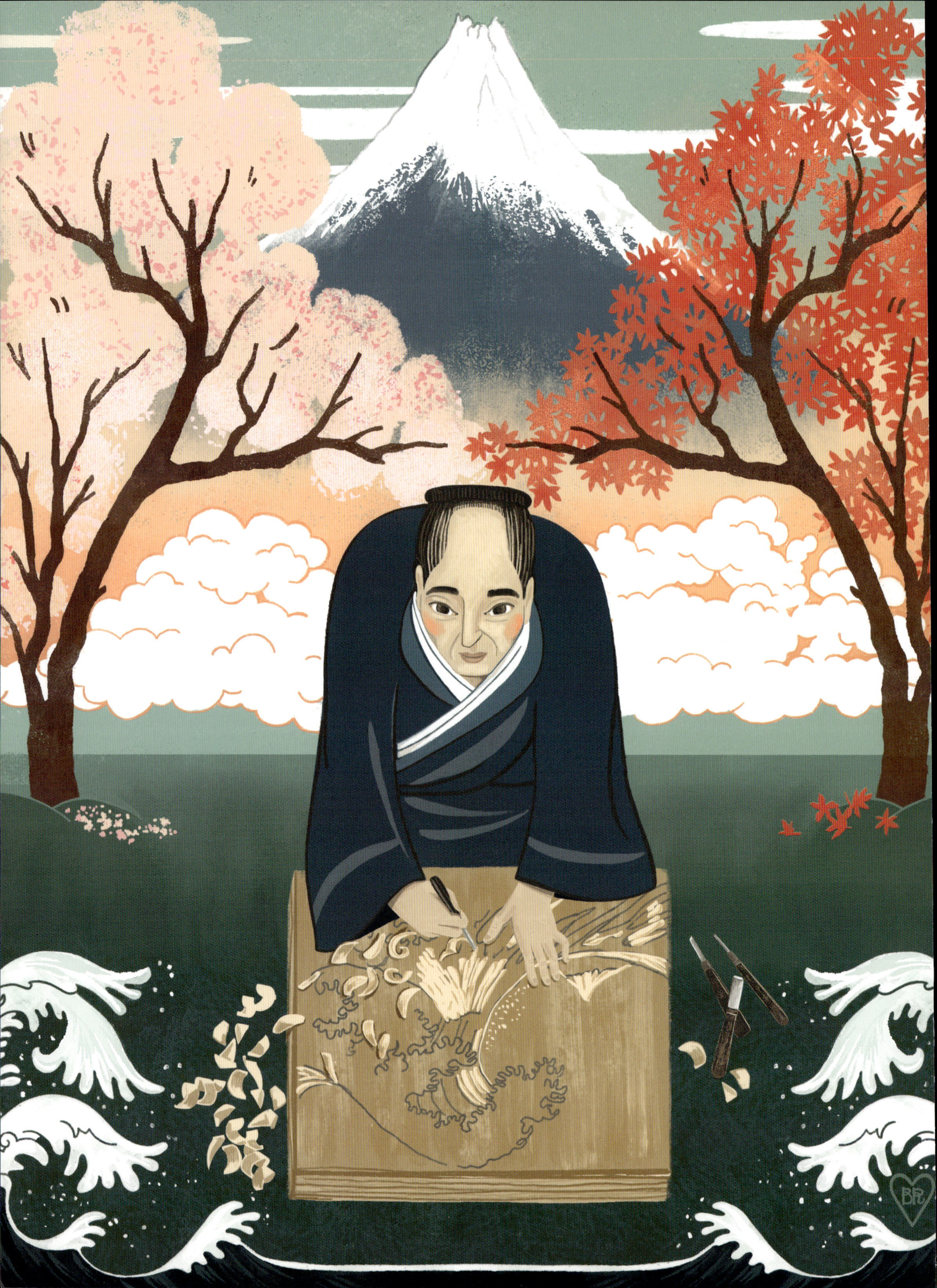

Katsushika Hokusai

Date of Birth: October 31, 1760 (approximate date)

Place of Birth: Edo, Japan

A MAN WITH MANY NAMES

Hokusai was born in the Katsushika district of Edo, which is now modern-day Tokyo. At the time, Edo was the biggest city in the world with a population of around one million people. Hokusai's childhood name was Tokitarō. Throughout his lifetime, he was known by at least thirty names. It was common for artists to use multiple names, and each of Hokusai's names was related to his changing artistic styles.

ARTISAN'S APPRENTICE

Born to a family of artisans, Hokusai's father was a mirror-maker. By age six, Hokusai began painting, and at fourteen, he became an apprentice to a wood-carver. By eighteen, Hokusai started working in Katsukawa Shunshō's art studio. There his name changed for the first time, and he was known as Shunrō.

ART FOR ALL

While working in Shunshō's studio, Hokusai gained popularity for his woodblock prints of famous actors. This type of art was called *ukiyo-e*, which means "pictures of the floating world." It was a popular art form, and artists made many copies of their own work through printmaking. People could buy prints for the price of a bowl of noodles, which was affordable for many.

By 1800, he took on his most known name, Katsushika Hokusai. As he got older, Hokusai created fewer portraits and more landscapes. He also started to paint pictures of everyday Japanese life.

ART TEACHER

Hokusai was one of Japan's most popular artists and a famous teacher. His youngest daughter, Katsushika Ōi, was one of his outstanding apprentices. During his lifetime, he taught over fifty students. In addition to training artists in his studio, Hokusai created a series of art manuals to teach people how to draw. These books included step-by-step directions for drawing different images.

VIEWS OF MOUNT FUJI

One of his most famous works was a series of thirty-six pictures of a mountain called Mount Fuji. He printed it in many different ways, and one of the pictures, *The Great Wave off Kanagawa*, was printed over eight thousand times! It became so popular that he added more prints to the series and eventually published *One Hundred Views of Mount Fuji*.

A PERSISTENT ARTIST

Although Hokusai had many successes, he faced some difficulties. He was hit by lightning, he had a stroke, and a fire destroyed his studio and artwork. Although he had to relearn how to paint, he never gave up and continued working until his death in 1849. Hokusai's last words were, "If heaven will afford me five more years of life, then I'll manage to become a true artist."

FAST FACT
He was known by at least thirty names throughout his lifetime.

Changing Landscapes

Create a series of changing landscape drawings.

MATERIALS

- 4 sheets of watercolor paper
- Pencil
- Pen or permanent marker
- Watercolor paint
- Paintbrushes
- Paint palette
- Water cup

VOCABULARY

LANDSCAPE: A picture of nature and the Earth's different landforms.

UKIYO-E: A style of art popular in Japan that depicted everyday life, people, and scenes.

PERSPECTIVE: The angle or direction you look at something.

ART CONNECTIONS

Hokusai inspired many artists worldwide, including Claude Monet and Vincent van Gogh. His most famous series was *One Hundred Views of Mount Fuji*. These prints show Mount Fuji from different viewpoints, including from a forest, village, lake, river, beach, and sea. He also painted the same view but during different seasons and times of the day. Monet did something similar with his series of paintings called *Haystacks*, where he painted the same **landscape** throughout the year.

Fig. 1: Find a landscape you want to capture.

Fig. 2: Draw your landscape.

Fig. 3: Add color to your landscape.

38 BE A CREATIVE CHANGEMAKER: A KIDS' ART ACTIVITY BOOK

Let's Get Started!

1: Hokusai was the first **ukiyo-e** artist to focus mainly on landscapes. His woodblock prints showed views of famous places throughout Japan. Think of a landscape you would like to focus on for your artwork. This landscape could be the view outside your window or a famous place you would like to visit. Find a photograph to reference if you cannot see your landscape while working.

For my example, I painted Crater Lake National Park in Oregon, US. **Fig. 1**

2: On watercolor paper, use a pencil to outline the plants, buildings, landforms, water, and sky of your landscape. Add any additional animals, people, or objects you see. Trace your drawing with a pen or permanent marker. **Fig. 2**

3: Use watercolor paint to begin adding color to your work. Consider how the weather and lighting conditions affect the colors you see. For example, you may notice that the sky changes color throughout the day. **Fig. 3**

4: Create a new drawing of the same landscape on a new sheet of paper. Think about changing your **perspective** or painting the landscape at a different time of the day. Notice how the composition, colors, and light differ from your original painting. **Fig. 4**

5: Create at least two more landscapes to add to your series.

You don't have to paint everything all in one day. Consider painting when the weather is slightly different or even during different seasons throughout the year. **Fig. 5**

Fig. 4: Change your perspective or draw the same landscape at a different time of day.

Fig. 5: Draw your landscape again when the weather changes or during different seasons.

TECHNIQUES & TIPS

- If you need a color you do not have, try mixing colors on a palette to create a new color. You can apply one watercolor wash onto your paper, then immediately blend a different color. This technique is known as painting wet-on-wet. See what happens when mixing one, two, three, or more colors.

- Throughout the day, you may see shifting shadows throughout your landscape. A shadow is a darker shade of color. If a tree is leaving a shadow on the grass, you can paint a darker green for the shadow. You can mix green with a little black to make a darker green. You can also paint one wash of green, and after it has dried, add more green on top. With each layer of paint, you will notice the colors appear darker. This method of layering watercolors is also known as glazing.

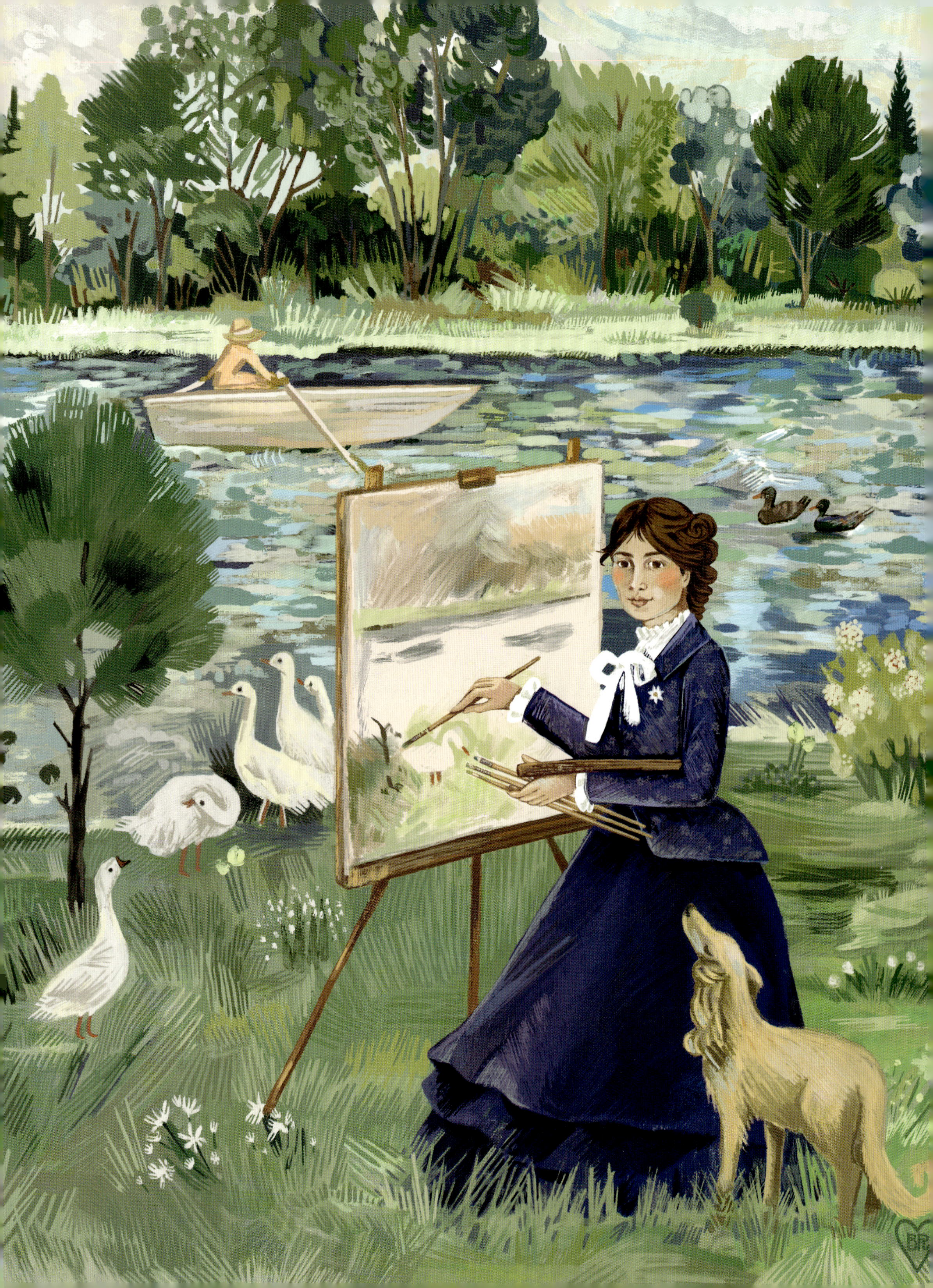

Berthe Morisot

Date of Birth: January 14, 1841

Place of Birth: Bourges, France

TALENTED SISTERS

Berthe and her sister Edma loved art and learned how to paint when they were young. Eventually, they traveled to Paris to learn more. They would visit the famous Louvre Museum to copy paintings and develop their skills. Soon, both sisters began taking lessons from a renowned landscape painter, Jean-Baptiste-Camille Corot.

PLEIN-AIR PAINTING

Corot liked to paint outside instead of in a studio. This way of painting is called en plein-air painting. By painting outside, the artist can see what they're painting and make it look more realistic. At the time, it was not common for people to paint outside in France, but Corot showed Berthe and Edma how to do it. Even though they were both good at painting, only Berthe continued her career as an artist.

THE PARIS SALON

In 1864, judges picked two of Berthe's paintings to display at a big art show in France called the Paris Salon. This juried art show began in 1667 and was France's most important annual art event. Berthe's work was well received, and she continued showing her art at the Salon for almost a decade.

LASTING FRIENDSHIP

In 1868, Berthe met a painter named Édouard Manet, and they became friends. They both admired each other's art and even painted each other. Édouard also introduced Berthe to a group of artists who would later be known as the Impressionists.

THE IMPRESSIONISTS

The Impressionists were a group of artists who painted differently than others at the time. They used bright colors, showed brushstrokes, and painted everyday things. Some people didn't like their art, thinking it looked messy and incomplete. But others like Berthe thought their new ideas, techniques, and approach were exciting.

In 1874, Berthe was a part of the first Impressionist show, which included the work of Claude Monet, Edgar Degas, Pierre-Auguste Renoir, and Camille Pissarro. The Impressionists continued developing their unique techniques and showing their art as a group until the mid-1880s.

HOME AND FAMILY LIFE

Berthe eventually married Édouard's younger brother, Eugène, who was also an artist. She continued her work and liked painting pictures of her family, including her sister, husband, and daughter Julie.

In 1892, Berthe had her first solo exhibition. Unfortunately, she passed away three years later at the age of fifty-five. Although Berthe achieved great success during her lifetime, many artworks were in her studio unseen. A year after Berthe's death, her friends and fellow Impressionist artists put together a retrospective with over three hundred paintings to share her talent.

FAST FACT

Berthe was one of the founding members of the Impressionism art movement.

Impressionist Painting

Paint an en plein-air landscape.

MATERIALS
- Stretched canvas
- Portable easel (optional)
- Pencil
- Acrylic paint
- Paintbrushes
- Paint palette
- Water cup

ART CONNECTIONS

Although each Impressionist painter had a unique style, their works had some things in common. One of those similarities was that they liked to paint everyday life outside. They called this *en plein air*, which is French for "in the open air." Impressionists would set their **easels** up outside and paint what they saw in front of them. They often used thick brushstrokes and bright colors to show how the light made everything look. The goal was not to make their paintings look realistic but to capture the **impression** of the moment.

VOCABULARY

EN PLEIN AIR: A French expression that translates to "in the open air." It describes painting outdoors while looking directly at your subject matter.

EASEL: A frame used to support a work of art while being painted or drawn.

IMPRESSION: A general idea, feeling, or opinion about something.

Fig. 1: Find an outdoor space to work.

Fig. 2: Sketch your scene.

Fig. 3: Paint the sky.

Let's Get Started!

1: Impressionist artists painted many outdoor scenes, including the countryside, city streets, gardens, and waterfronts.

Find a place where you can safely paint outdoors. This place may be outside your front door, in your backyard, or at a local park. Be sure to have an adult accompany you and bring your painting materials.

2: Once you are in that location, find an area to work. If you have a portable easel, set that up. Lay out your brushes, paint, and water. **Fig. 1**

3: Quickly use a pencil to sketch what you see. Use big shapes to lay things out without much attention to small details. **Fig. 2**

4: When painting outside, you must paint quickly to keep up with the changing daylight. The colors and light will change as the sun moves throughout the day. Begin with the sky and paint the position of the sun and clouds. Look carefully for the different colors you see. Notice that the sky is not always blue! **Fig. 3**

5: Begin to paint the land. Use thick brushstrokes and do not blend the colors. **Fig. 4**

6: Finish painting the other objects and subjects in your landscape. You are capturing a moment, so don't worry if animals or people have moved around. Use big, bold marks and don't focus on small details. **Fig. 5**

7: Compare your painting to what you see in front of you. Refine your work by adding additional details. Consider using small brushstrokes to paint leaves and blades of grass while adding any highlights and shadows you may have missed. Your painting does not need to look realistic. Instead, focus on capturing the moment. **Fig. 6**

TECHNIQUES & TIPS

- Impressionist artists used bright and bold colors. But when painting en plein air, you have less time to mix paint. Impressionists often painted with colors straight from the tube and even blended the colors on the canvas to save time.

- Impressionist artists would paint with an easel. An easel is a frame used to support a work of art while being painted or drawn. If you do not have access to a portable easel, bring a blanket or towel that you can sit on. Sit up with your legs bent and place your canvas between your knees. This position will help elevate your work so you can see the landscape while painting. Occasionally stop and hold your painting up to compare it side-by-side to your landscape.

Fig. 4: Paint the ground.

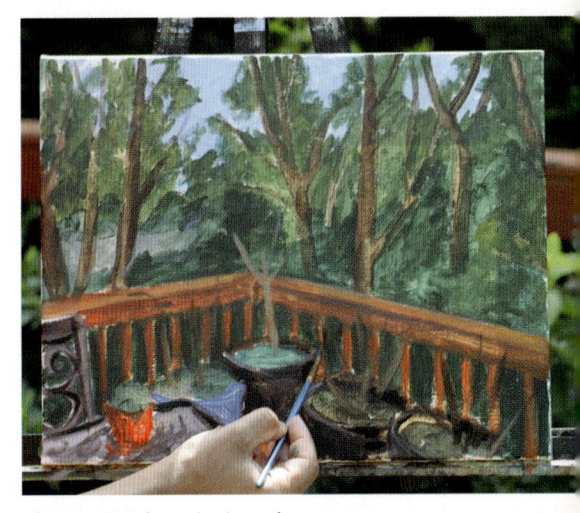

Fig. 5: Finish painting the scene.

Fig. 6: Refine the details.

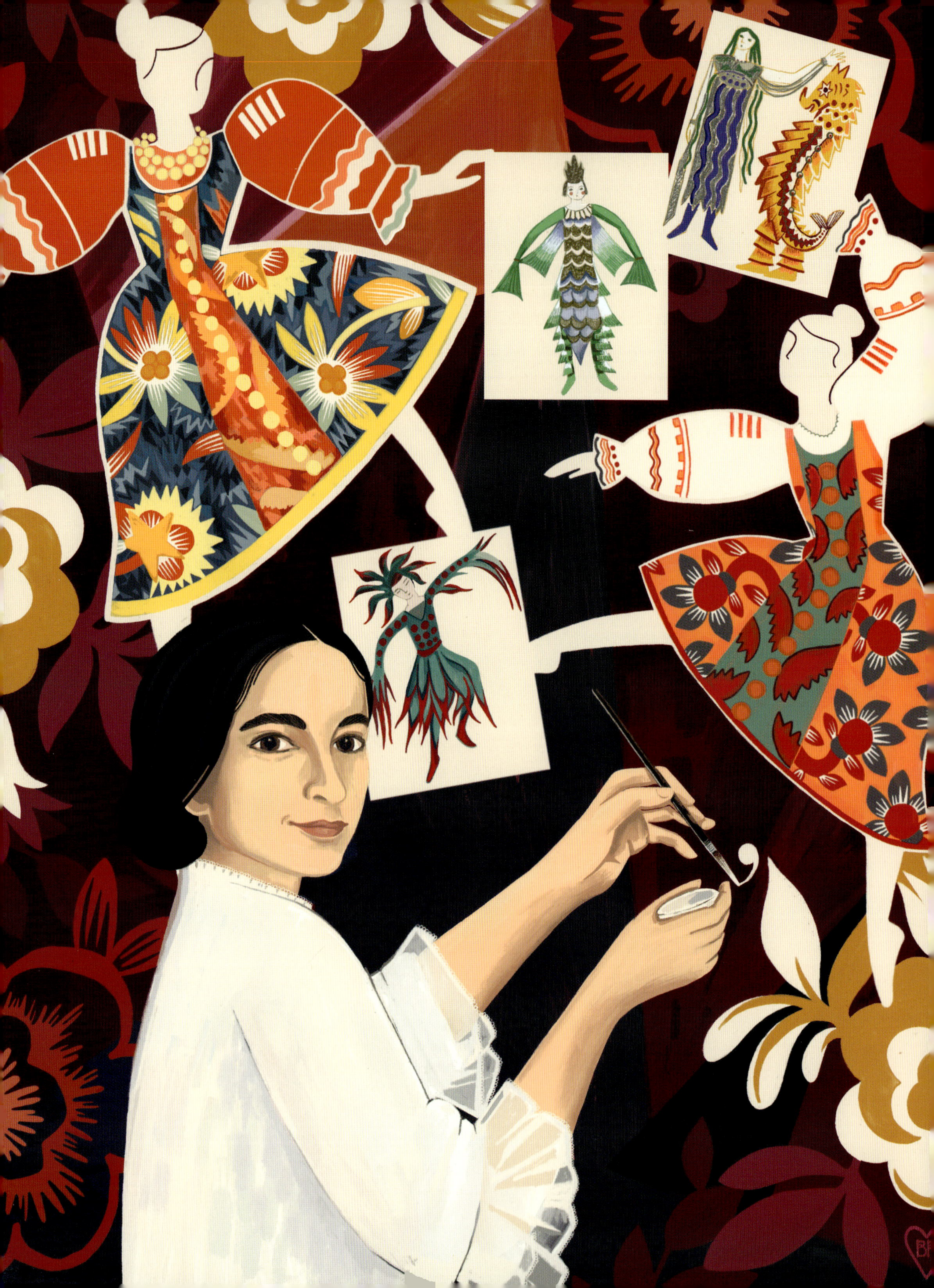

Natalia Sergeevna Goncharova

Date of Birth: 1881 (approximate date)

Place of Birth: Nagaevo, Tula Governorate, present-day Russia

YOUNG BEGINNINGS

Natalia was born in Nagaevo, a town in Russia, where she lived on her grandmother's estate. When she was ten, her family moved to a big city called Moscow. There, she started learning how to make sculptures with a local artist.

MOSCOW SCHOOL OF PAINTING, SCULPTURE, AND ARCHITECTURE

Natalia became a talented sculptor and went to the Moscow School of Painting, Sculpture, and Architecture. She fell in love with another student there named Mikhail Larionov. They started making art together and showed their work at many important art exhibitions.

A STYLE OF HER OWN

Natalia started making her own new style of painting. She drew inspiration from traditional Russian folk art and included elements of luboks in her work. Luboks were popular Russian prints, similar to comic strips today. But instead of painting objects realistically, she began to abstract them. Her style was very different from other artists at the time.

CONTROVERSIAL FIGURE

Natalia continued to push cultural boundaries and started doing things that people thought were strange at the time. She would often wear men's clothing and sometimes go out with designs painted on her face and body. She and Mikhail believed that art should be a part of everyday life, and their actions made the two controversial. Some of her paintings were so shocking that in 1910 police took them away.

EVERYTHINGISM

Natalia and Mikhail also created a new style of art called Rayonism, inspired by science. This art was all about showing movement and energy. Rayonism focused on deconstructing light, and many raylike lines appeared in their work.

During her lifetime, Natalia had lots of different styles of art that she explored. In 1913 she had her first solo show in Moscow with over seven hundred works of art displayed. Her work was so diverse that a writer said her art was like "everythingism."

Later, Natalia and Mikhail moved to Paris where Natalia started making theater costumes and sets. She became famous for her designs and worked on many ballets and operas.

PERSISTENT PAINTER

Later, Natalia was diagnosed with rheumatoid arthritis. This condition made it challenging to create art with her hands. But Natalia found ways to wrap paintbrushes around her arms and continued to paint. Natalia and Mikhail eventually married after being together for over fifty years. The couple had a big show of all their art not long after. A year later, Natalia passed away in Paris at the age of eighty-one.

FAST FACT

Her art style was described as "everythingism."

Costume Design

Design a series of costumes inspired by your aesthetic.

MATERIALS
- Card stock paper
- Pencil
- Pen or permanent marker
- Colored pencils or markers
- Scissors

ART CONNECTIONS

Natalia made many designs for ballet and theater shows. Some of her most famous **costumes** and sets were for *The Golden Cockerel* and *The Firebird*. Just like with her paintings, Natalia's use of color and pattern was thoughtful and innovative. Her designs were modern, but she also included traditional Russian elements. Although her style changed, she maintained a unique **aesthetic**. Aesthetics are what people consider to be beautiful. Each artist's aesthetic is different and influences their work.

VOCABULARY

COSTUME: The clothing people wear during a specific time or for a particular event.

AESTHETIC: What we consider to be beautiful.

Let's Get Started!

1: In this activity, you will create a series of paper costumes for a performance. Begin by thinking of a live performance you have seen. It could be a play at your school, a ballet you attended at a theater, or a musical you watched on TV. Think about one character in that performance whose costumes you will design.

For example, I will create a series of costumes for Clara from *The Nutcracker* ballet.

2: Draw a model for your character on card stock paper. You can make them look however you want. Add details to their face, hands, and feet. **Fig. 1**

3: Create a stand for your character. Use a pencil to draw a semicircle on the bottom behind the feet. In the center, draw a short vertical line on the bottom. Find a blank space on your paper to draw another semicircle, a similar size to the one you previously drew. In the center, along the top, draw a short vertical line. **Fig. 1**

4: Trace your drawing with a pen or permanent marker. Use colored pencils or markers to add color to your model and stand. **Fig. 2**

5: Use scissors to cut out your model and stand. Carefully cut out the notches at the top and bottom of the semicircles. **Fig. 3**

(continued)

Fig. 1: Draw a model and stand.

Fig. 2: Add color.

Fig. 3: Cut out your model and stand.

Fig. 4: Trace your model onto another paper.

Fig. 5: Draw your costume design and add tabs and color.

Fig. 6: Place your model in the stand.

Fig. 7: Cut and attach the costume by folding the tabs over the figure.

Fig. 8 and Fig. 9: Create more costume designs!

48   BE A CREATIVE CHANGEMAKER: A KIDS' ART ACTIVITY BOOK

6: Place your model onto a sheet of paper and use a pencil to trace the outside edge. **Fig. 4**

7: Think about a specific scene in the performance you selected in step 1. Consider what type of costume your character wears during that scene.

Reflect on your own aesthetic and style. What type of clothes do you like to wear? What colors and patterns make up your wardrobe? How can you use these elements as inspiration for a costume?

Once you have an idea, draw your costume design on top of your traced figure. **Fig. 5**

8: Draw small rectangles along the outside of your costume. You will use these tabs to attach the clothing to your model. **Fig. 5**

9: Trace your drawing with a permanent marker before adding color using pencils or markers.

I chose to design the outfit that Clara wears on the night she receives the nutcracker. Because it is a party, I wanted to make a fancy dress. My personal aesthetic is very colorful, and I wear a lot of patterns, which I included in my design. **Fig. 5**

10: Attach the separated semicircle to your figure by sliding the notches together. **Fig. 6**

11: Use scissors to cut out your costume, leaving the tabs attached. Place your costume on top of your figure. Fold the tabs over to attach the outfit. **Fig. 7**

12: Follow steps 6 through 10 to create additional costumes for your character! **Fig. 8** and **Fig. 9**

TECHNIQUES & TIPS

- Add additional elements to your costumes. These pieces can include hats, jewelry, and shoes.
- Imagine using your costume in a theater production. Write a script starring the character you created. Design and build a set using a large box. You can paint the inside and create moving pieces with cardboard. You can also make additional characters and props. Consider performing your script for friends and family!

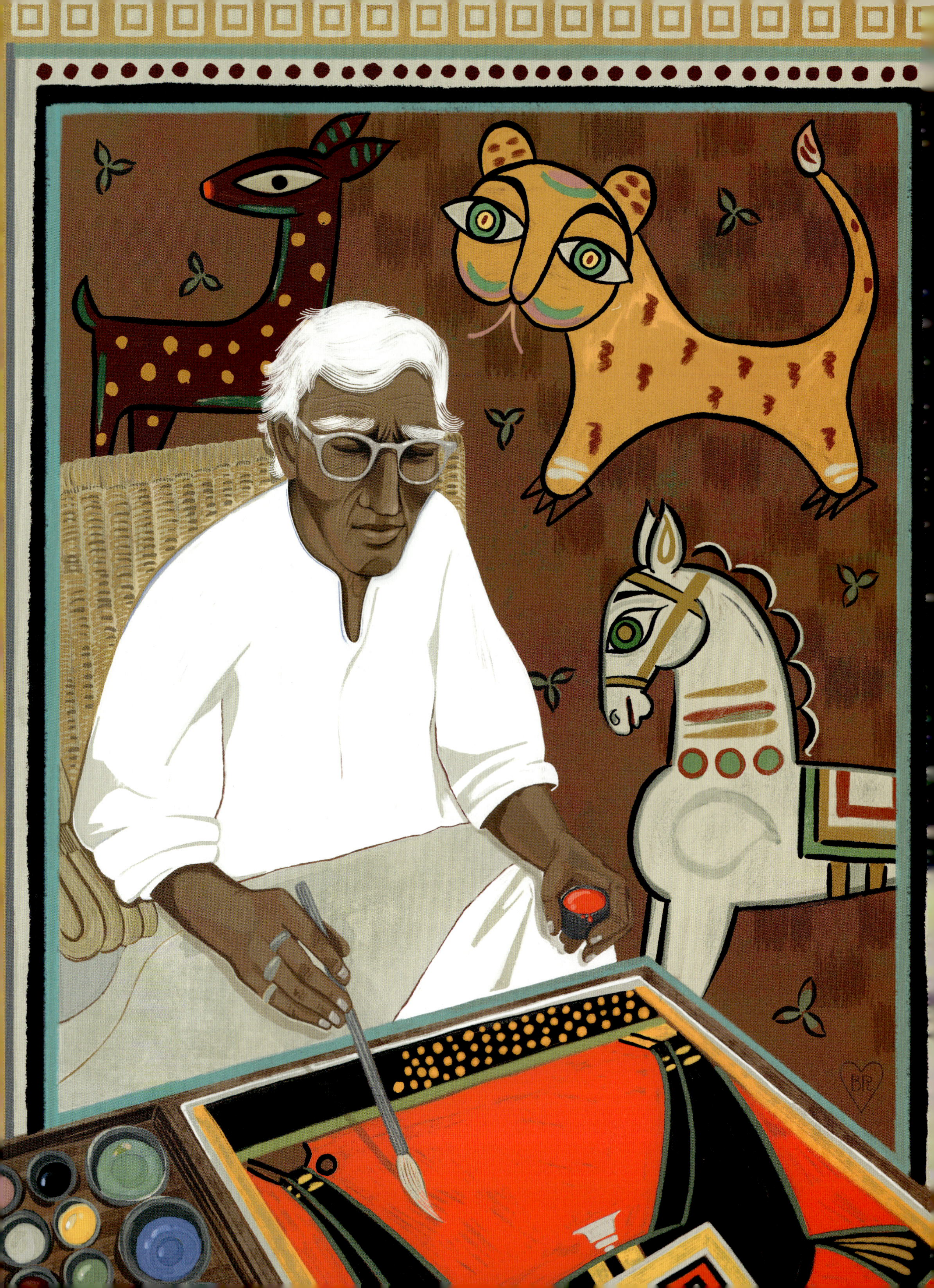

Jamini Roy

Date of Birth: April 11, 1887

Place of Birth: Beliatore, present-day India

A COMMUNITY OF ARTISTS

Jamini was born in a village called Beliatore in present-day India. When he was young, he was interested in the work of a community of artisans called Patuas. They made paintings on long pieces of paper called scroll paintings and would travel to other villages and sing songs about the stories in the paintings. Jamini liked art so much that he decided to attend art school in a large city called Kolkata.

A CHANGE IN STYLE

While in school, Jamini learned how to paint like European painters. His first paintings looked very realistic and had some similar qualities to a painting style called Impressionism. After he finished school, he began a successful career painting pictures of people and landscapes. But later on, he didn't want to paint like that anymore. He tried new styles and materials and found inspiration in Kalighat and Bengali folk paintings.

KALIGHAT PAINTING

Kalighat paintings were a unique type of art that started in the 1800s in eastern India. The style began near the Kalighat Kali Temple in Kolkata. Artists made these paintings and sold them to people visiting the temple who wanted unique souvenirs. The paintings showed Hindu gods, mythological characters, and other themes. Kalighat artists usually painted one scene and used bright colors, simple shapes, and bold outlines. This style was similar to the Patua scrolls that Jamini liked when he was a child.

A NEW VISUAL LANGUAGE

Jamini wanted to make art different from what he learned in school and represent his culture. Instead of painting on canvas, he painted on other materials such as woven mats and cloth. He also started to paint pictures of everyday people and animals. He kept trying new styles, and his paintings became simplified and more colorful.

A NATIONAL TREASURE

Jamini's art was so good that he won many honors for it. In 1954 he was given the Padma Bhushan, an important award in India. Later he was selected as a fellow of the National Academy of Art, and they held a special ceremony for him.

Jamini passed away when he was eighty-five. After he died, the Indian government declared Jamini Roy a national treasure artist, or a navratna of Indian art. The navratnas are considered the "Nine Gems of Indian art." In 1972 India made a law called The Antiquities and Art Treasures Act to protect navratnas' art. Because Jamini's art is so important, it has to stay in India. Today, you can only see most of his paintings if you visit India.

FAST FACT

His artwork is considered a national treasure of India.

Animal Motifs

Paint an animal motif.

MATERIALS
- Construction paper
- Pencil
- Permanent marker
- Ruler
- Tempera paint
- Paintbrushes
- Paint palette
- Water cup
- Colored pencils

ART CONNECTIONS

Jamini was a popular painter, and many people desired to own his art. Because he wanted his art to be affordable, Jamini started making more paintings. To help him, he also taught his son Amiya how to paint. They worked together in the studio, using similar **motifs**. Motifs are a repeating element found in designs. These repeating elements can include shapes, patterns, subjects, and themes. One common subject in Jamini's motif paintings was animals. Although they painted many different animals, their bodies and designs were usually similar. Amiya often started the paintings, but Jamini always added the final details.

VOCABULARY

MOTIF: A repeating element found in designs, which includes shapes, patterns, subjects, themes, and more.

PROFILE: An outline of an object turned to the side.

Fig. 1: Draw a profile of an animal.

Fig. 2: Draw a border around the edge of the paper.

Fig. 3: Add a motif and details to the background.

Let's Get Started!

1: Select a piece of colored construction paper. Lighter colors will be easier to draw and paint on.

2: One common subject repeated in Jamini's work was animals. He painted birds, elephants, lions, horses, cows, cats, and other animals native to his country of India.

Think of an animal that lives in your country. Draw that animal's **profile** (side) in the center of your paper. Keep your drawing simple. Use a permanent marker to trace your drawing.

I chose to draw my dog. **Fig. 1**

3: Draw lines around the edges of your paper to create a border. You can choose to add shapes and designs inside to create a motif. Use a permanent marker to trace your border.

Since my dog likes to play fetch, I added tennis balls inside my border. **Fig. 2**

4: Draw a motif in the background. Consider using geometric lines and shapes to create a unique design around your animal. You can also add additional details to your background. Use a permanent marker to trace your motif.

For my motif I decided to add small leaves in the background and dog bones. I also added a water bowl as an additional detail. **Fig. 3**

5: Paint your animal. The colors do not need to be realistic. You can use colors straight from the containers or mix your own. Be sure to paint the entire animal. **Fig. 4**

6: Paint the border and details around your animal. You can leave most of the background the color of your paper. **Fig. 5**

7: Many of Jamini's paintings include bold outlines. Once the paint has dried, outline your painting with colored pencils. Try using different colors for the various pieces and adding final details. **Fig. 6**

TECHNIQUES & TIPS

- Jamini used simplified shapes and bold outlines in much of his work. As a result, many of his animal paintings look two-dimensional. Jamini's animal paintings often did not include an environment. Instead of a scene, he painted many colorful shapes, patterns, designs, and borders. Try to use geometric lines and shapes to create your motifs!

- Jamini often worked with local materials and painted on woven mats, wood, and cloth. Instead of painting on construction paper, you can also experiment with painting on different surfaces. Look for items around your home that you could paint on. Consider using recycled items such as cardboard or old clothing.

Fig. 4: Paint your animal.

Fig. 5: Paint the border and details around your animal.

Fig. 6: Outline your painting with colored pencils.

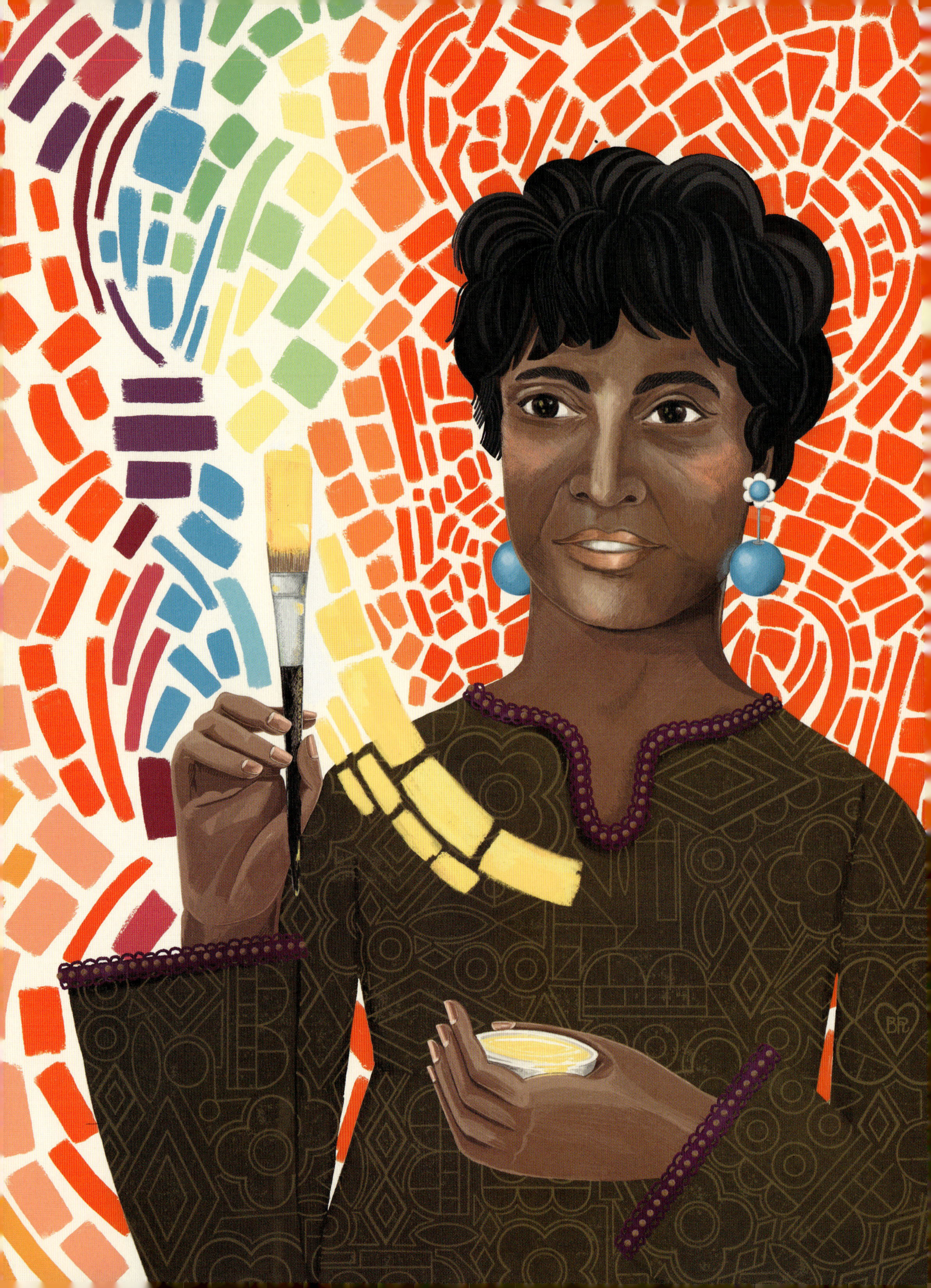

Alma Thomas

Date of Birth: September 22, 1891

Place of Birth: Columbus, Georgia, US

A RED BRICK HOME

Born in Columbus, Georgia, Alma was the oldest of four sisters. Her dad was a businessman, and her mom made clothes. During that time, some areas in the US had unjust laws that separated and treated Black people unfairly. Because of those laws, Alma's family moved to Washington, DC, in search of better opportunities and education. They bought a red-brick home close to the White House, and Alma lived there for the rest of her life.

ART EDUCATION

When Alma went to high school, she immediately fell in love with art. Following her passion, Alma studied art at a local college called Howard University. In 1924, she became the first person at the school to graduate with a fine arts degree.

TEACHING ARTIST

After college, she became an art teacher at a local junior high school. Alma organized art clubs, exhibitions, and lectures for her students. She believed art could empower people and she inspired many young artists during her career.

While teaching, Alma continued learning and making her paintings. She attended graduate school at Columbia University, studied abroad in Europe, and attended painting classes at American University. Alma also exhibited her paintings in many group shows. Her art was initially realistic, but she made more abstract paintings as she got older.

FAST FACT
Alma was an art teacher for over thirty years.

RETIREMENT AND A NEW DAWN

After working for over thirty years, Alma retired from teaching and had more time to paint. While looking out the window of her home, Alma noticed the light coming through the leaves onto her flower garden. Inspired, she began to explore the power of light and color in her work. She deconstructed what she saw into broad paint strokes and rows of bright colors. This series of Earth paintings became an important point in her artistic career.

A CURRENT RETROSPECTIVE

In 1966, Howard University wanted to exhibit a retrospective of Alma's art. A retrospective is a collection of work that someone has created in the past. But instead of showing her older paintings, Alma shared her new series of Earth paintings. Her distinct style became instantly popular, and she started to get a lot of recognition for her art.

REACHING FOR THE STARS

The moon landing in 1969 fascinated Alma, and space became a central theme in her paintings. Instead of finding inspiration from the Earth, she began to look to the cosmos. During her final years of painting, Alma imagined stars, distant planets, and space travel.

"LOOK AT ME NOW"

At age eighty-one, Alma was the first African American woman to have a solo exhibition at the Whitney Museum of American Art. She told *The New York Times*, "One of the things we couldn't do was go into museums, let alone think of hanging our pictures there. My, times have changed. Just look at me now."

Alma passed away in 1978. She was a lifelong learner, educator, and artist whose work continues to inspire today.

Colors of the Cosmos

Find inspiration in the colors and beauty you see around you.

MATERIALS
- Watercolor paper
- Watercolor paint
- Paint palette
- Flat paintbrushes
- Water cup
- Pencil
- Canvas
- Tempera or acrylic paint

VOCABULARY

COSMOS: The universe as a whole.

ABSTRACT ART: Art that does not attempt to represent reality and uses visual elements such as shapes, lines, colors, and textures to express ideas.

ART CONNECTIONS

Alma found beauty and inspiration all around her, including in the **cosmos**. The cosmos is the universe as a whole. That includes all that is found in nature here on Earth and everything out in space. From her window, Alma looked out at the holly tree and found beauty in the light shining through the leaves. Her paint palette included the colors of the flower gardens near her home, and she created exciting paintings inspired by the NASA space launch. Wherever she was, Alma saw the beauty in everything and captured that beauty within her art.

Throughout time, many artists have been inspired by their surroundings. Sometimes artists create realistic representations while others' work is abstract. **Abstract art** does not try to picture the real world. It uses visual elements such as shapes, lines, colors, and textures to express ideas. In her abstract paintings, Alma captured the beauty she saw around her through vibrant colors.

Fig. 1: Find a source of inspiration.

Fig. 2: Plan your painting with a watercolor sketch.

Fig. 3: Use a flat brush to paint rows of color.

Let's Get Started!

1: Find a source of inspiration for your abstract painting. Like Alma, look for the beauty in what is around you. This could be the sun shining through leaves out of a window or a yellow moon that fills the night sky. **Fig. 1**

2: Before painting on canvas, Alma would plan her work with a watercolor painting.

Look at your source of inspiration and find the beauty in the different colors, lines, and shapes. Create a sketch using watercolor paint to capture those elements. Instead of blending your paint, use a flat brush to paint patches of colors.

You can create as many sketches as you need before moving on to your final painting. **Fig. 2**

3: Once you have planned your painting, use a pencil to sketch the shapes onto a canvas.

4: Mix tempera or acrylic colors on a paint palette before using a flat brush to paint rows of color. Start with one color before moving on to the next. You can also use different-size paintbrushes. **Fig. 3**

5: Hold your brush parallel to the paper as you apply thick, rectangular strokes of color. **Fig. 4**

6: Continue mixing colors on a palette before applying them to the canvas. Be sure to look at your source of inspiration and watercolor sketch as you work. **Fig. 5**

7: When you are done, look for other sources of inspiration and create more paintings. This might include plants or planets!

After painting the view from my window, I was inspired by images taken from the James Webb Space Telescope to make a new painting. **Fig. 6**

Fig. 4: Paint more rows of color.

Fig. 5: Complete your painting.

Fig. 6: Find more sources of inspiration to paint!

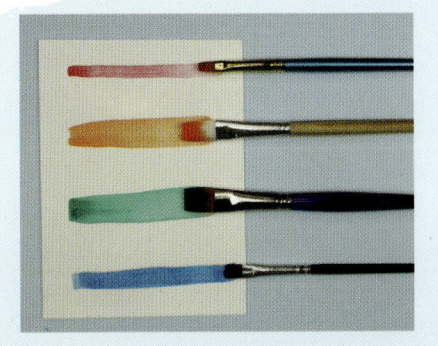

TECHNIQUES & TIPS

- When you look closely at Alma's later work, her brushstrokes look like bricks or tiles. The closer you are to the painting, the clearer the brushstrokes are.

- Paintbrushes come in many different shapes and sizes. For this activity, it is best to use a flat paintbrush. Flat paintbrushes have a straight tip and look rectangular. They are great to use when painting straight edges. Other paintbrush shapes include round, bright, filbert, angle, and fan.

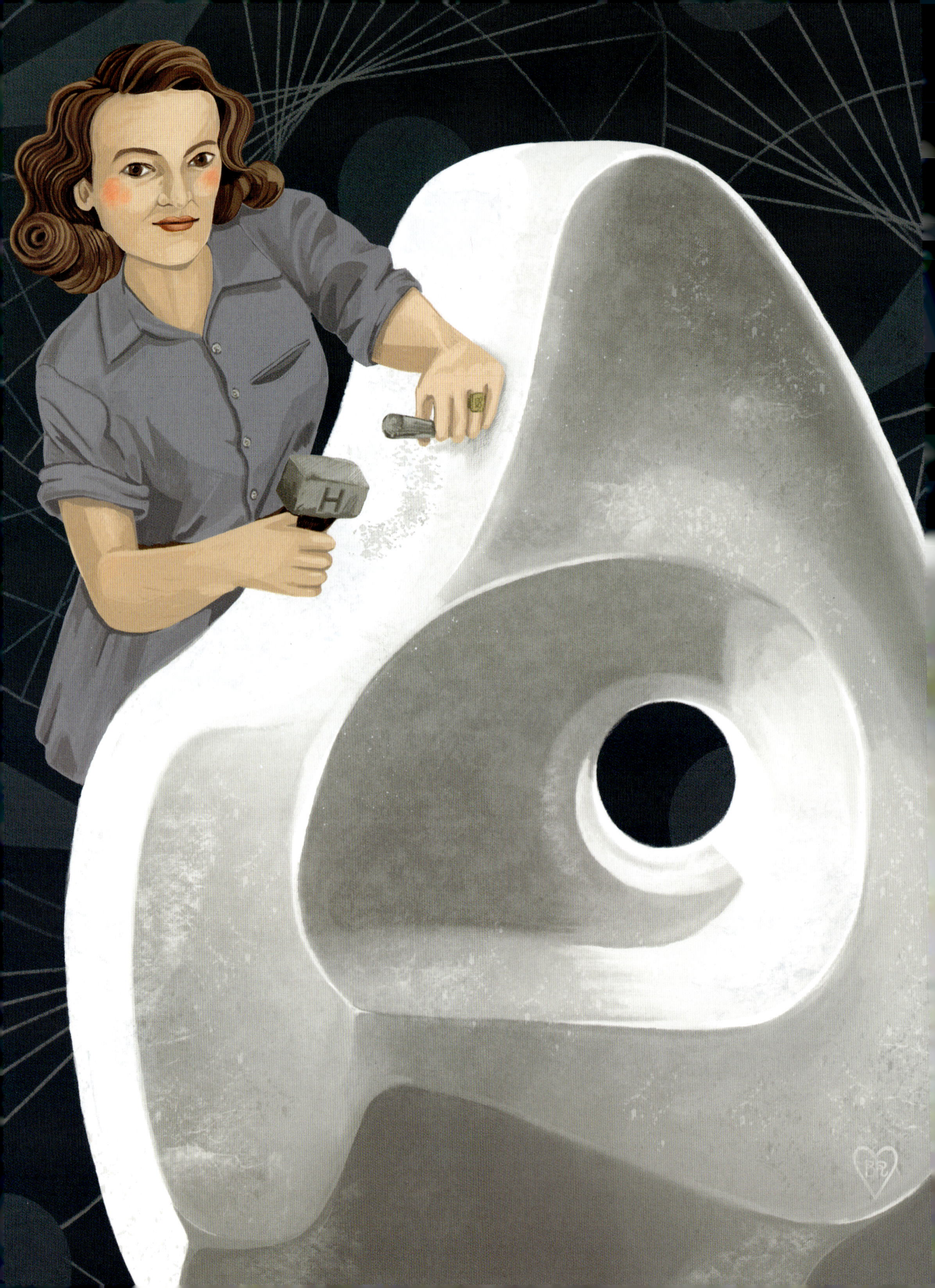

Barbara Hepworth

Date of Birth: January 10, 1903

Place of Birth: Wakefield, England

SCHOLARSHIPS

Barbara was the oldest of four kids. As a child, she loved traveling with her dad during his work trips as a civil engineer. When Barbara was sixteen, she won an art school scholarship and finished the course in one year instead of two. Later, she got another scholarship to attend the Royal College of Art in London.

STONEMASONRY

After graduation, Barbara stayed in London for a year before traveling to Italy. In Rome, she learned how to carve stones. Stone-carving was traditionally a skill for a stonemason rather than an artist. But she found ways to use this new technique in her work. Barbara returned to London, where she exhibited a series of figures and animals carved from stone.

GEOMETRIC FORMS

Over time, Barbara's work became more abstract. Her sculptures mainly consisted of geometric forms such as spheres, cones, and cylinders. She also began working on a much larger scale; many pieces could fill entire rooms. Barbara's innovative sculptures made her a leader in modern art, and she met many other famous artists. Eventually, Barbara married one of them named Ben Nicholson, with whom she shared an art studio in London.

RELOCATION

When World War II started, the couple feared a military attack on London. So they moved to a seaside town called St Ives. Because the sculptures were so large, they had to leave them behind. In St Ives, Barbara no longer had the space or materials to create her large stone sculptures, so she started drawing instead. Unfortunately, bombs destroyed their London studio and many of Barbara's sculptures.

NEW INSPIRATION

Barbara eventually purchased a home with a garden where she could work and display her sculptures. She called it Trewyn Studio. The surrounding rock forms, changing tides, and bay curves inspired her. Barbara also began creating work in bronze. This new material allowed Barbara to make small cast copies of her work, and people worldwide bought her bronze sculptures.

DAME COMMANDER OF THE BRITISH EMPIRE

Barbara's art was so significant that she was appointed Dame Commander of the Order of the British Empire and was the first female trustee of the Tate Gallery in London. Barbara continued to create and exhibit her art until her untimely death after an accidental fire at her studio.

FAST FACT
She made over six hundred sculptures.

Subtractive Sculpture

Carve an abstract form.

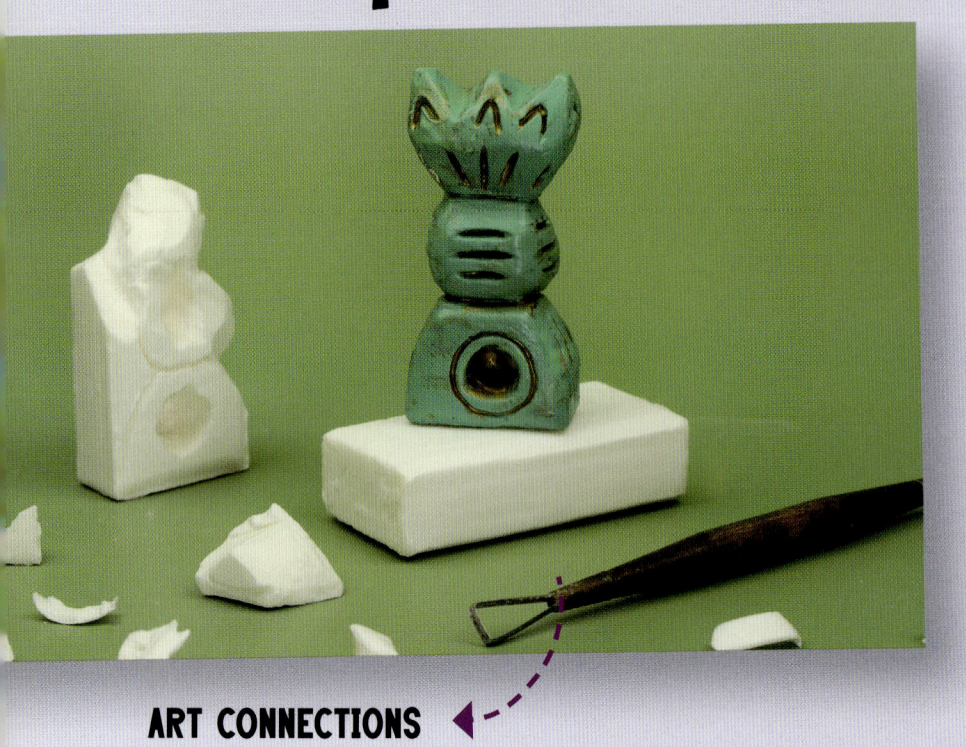

MATERIALS
- Paper
- Pencil
- Soap bar
- Clay loop tool
- Water cup or wet sponge
- Acrylic paint
- Paintbrushes
- Paint palette

VOCABULARY

CARVING: When you cut or carve into a material.

GEOMETRIC SHAPES: Mathematical shapes with a specific amount of points, curves, and lines (e.g., squares, rectangles, triangles, and circles).

ORGANIC SHAPES: Similar to shapes you find in nature, often with uneven features and curves.

ART CONNECTIONS

Barbara carved many of her sculptures by hand. A **carving** is when you cut into a material. Carving is a subtractive method of sculpture because you are taking material away. Some of Barbara's sculptures contain only **geometric shapes** like spheres and cylinders. Other sculptures used **organic shapes** and looked like things she found in nature, such as shells and rocks. Barbara also made holes and cutouts in her sculptures to let light show through. She even tied strings through some of the holes to connect different parts. Barbara described it as representing the pull she felt toward the beauty of the landscape.

Fig. 1: Draw and combine shapes on a sheet of paper to create a unique abstract design.

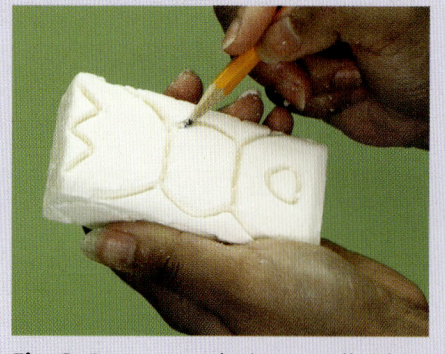

Fig. 2: Draw your design on all sides of a soap bar.

Fig. 3: Carve the corners and edges of your sculpture.

BE A CREATIVE CHANGEMAKER: A KIDS' ART ACTIVITY BOOK

Let's Get Started!

1: Throughout her life, Barbara's sculptures consisted of a combination of geometric and organic shapes. Think about the different shapes that interest you. Like Barbara, you may find inspiration in your environment. Draw and combine shapes on a sheet of paper to create a unique abstract design. **Fig. 1**

2: We will carve into a soap bar to create our sculpture. Using your sketch from step 1, draw your design on the front and back of your soap bar. Think about what it will look like from all angles as you draw on the sides. **Fig. 2**

3: Use a loop tool to carve the large areas around the corners and edges. **Fig. 3**

4: Continue to carve and refine the form of your sculpture. Use a pencil to add small details. Make sure you look at and carve your sculpture from all sides. **Fig. 4**

5: Dip your fingers in water or use a wet sponge to smooth the surface of your sculpture. **Fig. 5**

6: Use acrylic to paint your sculpture. Consider painting any indents and holes a different color to highlight the details. **Fig. 6**

Fig. 4: Refine your sculpture.

Fig. 5: Smooth your sculpture.

Fig. 6: Paint your sculpture.

TECHNIQUES & TIPS

- Barbara worked mainly with wood and stone. This process involves many sharp tools and is very time-consuming. A soap bar for this activity is best because it is easy to carve, but you may also use clay, plaster, or foam.

- It is important to look at your sculpture from all sides while carving. A sculpture is three-dimensional, and people will look all around it.

BARBARA HEPWORTH

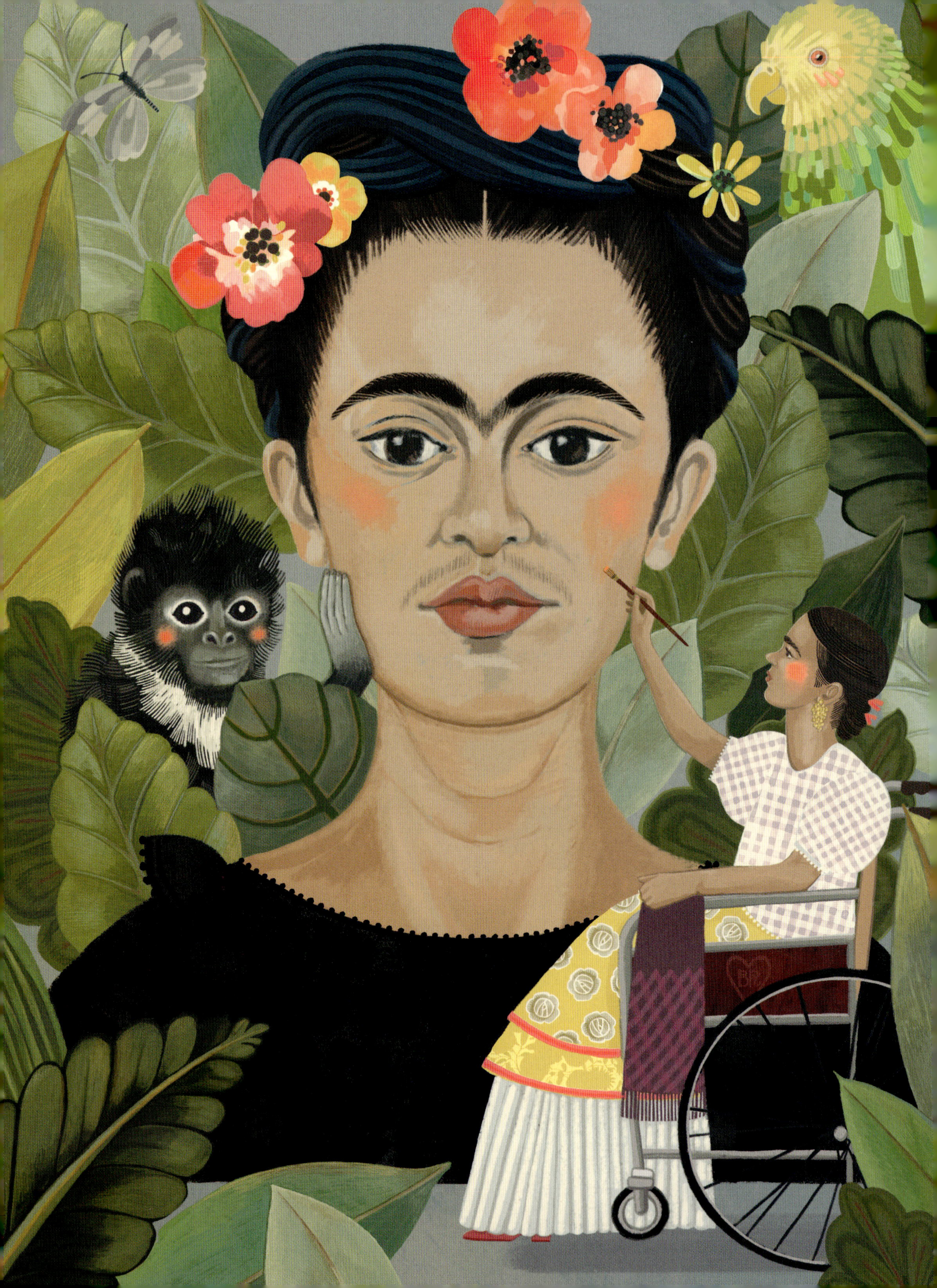

Frida Kahlo

Date of Birth: July 6, 1907

Place of Birth: Coyoacán, Mexico City, Mexico

FAST FACT
She lived most of her life in the same house she was born, La Casa Azul.

MEXICAN ROOTS

Magdalena Carmen Frida Kahlo Calderón was born in La Casa Azul, a blue house outside Mexico City. Today, she is more commonly known as Frida Kahlo. Her father was a German photographer who had moved to Mexico, and her mother was of Indigenous and Spanish descent. She was very proud of her heritage. Looking closely, you can see the Mexican flag and other cultural symbols in many of her paintings.

CHALLENGING STEREOTYPES

When she was six, Frida got very sick with polio, and one of her legs became shorter and thinner than the other. Although she would wear long pants and skirts to hide her leg, she didn't let her sickness stop her from being active. Frida played soccer, swam, and even wrestled! Playing sports was not usual for girls then, and she continued to challenge gender stereotypes. She even posed for a family portrait in a three-piece suit, traditionally worn by men.

INTRODUCTION TO ART

When she was younger, Frida liked to spend time with her dad in his photography studio and sometimes took drawing classes. She was also fascinated by science and wanted to study medicine. But one day, when she was on her way home from school, her bus got into a big accident. She was severely hurt and had to stay in the hospital for a long time. She was placed in a full-body cast and would use a wheelchair throughout her life. While in bed recovering, Frida began painting designs on her casts and started to paint using a special easel.

"THE SUBJECT I KNOW BEST"

Frida painted the world as she saw it through her own eyes. Although she created pictures of many things, Frida became most known for her self-portraits. Of the approximately 143 paintings she created, 55 were self-portraits! Through these self-portraits, Frida began to explore the different parts of her identity. She painted about her experiences, relationships, culture, politics, and the pain of her injuries. Frida once said, "I paint myself because I am so often alone, and I am the subject I know best."

ROMANTIC RELATIONSHIPS

Frida had romantic relationships with men and women, the longest being with muralist Diego Rivera. They had a very passionate yet unstable relationship, divorcing once and marrying twice. Although she could not have children, the couple had many pets, such as cats, dogs, birds, and even monkeys. She included some of her pets in her paintings.

LA CASA AZUL

Although Frida painted for most of her life, she did not get much attention for her work while alive. Despite the lack of recognition and ongoing health issues, she never stopped painting. Even when she was very sick, she went to her final art show in an ambulance and lay on a bed at the gallery. Unfortunately, a few months later, Frida passed away at forty-seven. Today, La Casa Azul is a museum where visitors can see her art, studio, and home.

Symbolic Self-Portrait

Paint a self-portrait that symbolizes different parts of your identity.

MATERIALS
- Mirror or photo of yourself
- Paper or canvas
- Pencil
- Paint (watercolor, tempera, or acrylic)
- Paintbrushes
- Paint palette
- Water cup
- Colored pencils (optional)

VOCABULARY

SYMBOLS: Using images that represent something else.

IDENTITY: The different parts about yourself that make you who you are.

OBSERVATION: Looking at something very carefully.

ART CONNECTIONS

Frida often explored her experiences and reality through the use of **symbols**. A symbol is an image that represents something else. During her life, she used many symbols to describe different parts of her **identity**. In one of her first self-portraits, *Time Flies*, Frida used red, white, and green to represent the Mexican flag and her heritage. Later she painted a broken column in place of her spine to symbolize her pain.

Fig. 1: Look in a mirror and draw yourself.

Fig. 2: Add images and symbols representing different parts of your identity.

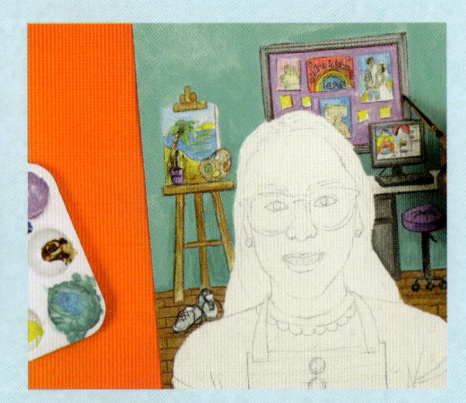

Fig. 3: Paint your background.

Let's Get Started!

1: Frida's self-portraits detail her experiences and identity. Our identities are the different parts of ourselves that make us who we are. Many things make us unique, and we will express them in this self-portrait painting.

2: One part of our identity includes our appearance. Begin by drawing yourself from **observation**. Observation means looking at something very carefully. You will have to look in a mirror or use a photo to paint yourself from observation.

I focused on my face, but you may choose to draw your entire body. **Fig. I**

3: Who you are is more than your appearance and includes many different things. Your identity includes your interests, talents, skills, abilities, languages, thoughts, beliefs, values, cultures, religions, traditions, hopes, feelings, and more!

Think about which of these is most important to you. Use images and symbols in your background and accessories to represent the different pieces of your identity. **Fig. 2**

4: Start by painting your background. **Fig. 3**

5: Paint yourself, your clothing, and your accessories. **Fig. 4**

6: Use a small paintbrush or colored pencils to refine your work and add tiny details or patterns.

I used colored pencils to draw eyelashes, eyebrows, and hair strands around my face. **Fig. 5**

Fig. 4: Paint yourself.

Fig. 5: Use a small paintbrush or colored pencils to add details.

TECHNIQUES & TIPS

- Our skin color is unique, and not everyone's skin color matches the paint from a bottle. When painting your skin, mix and paint small dots on the back of your hand to try and match your skin color.

- Human skin comes in many shades of brown. You can create brown by mixing the three primary colors: red, yellow, and blue. You can also make brown by mixing complementary colors such as red and green, blue and orange, or yellow and violet. You can then add black to make your skin color darker or white to make your skin color lighter.

FRIDA KAHLO

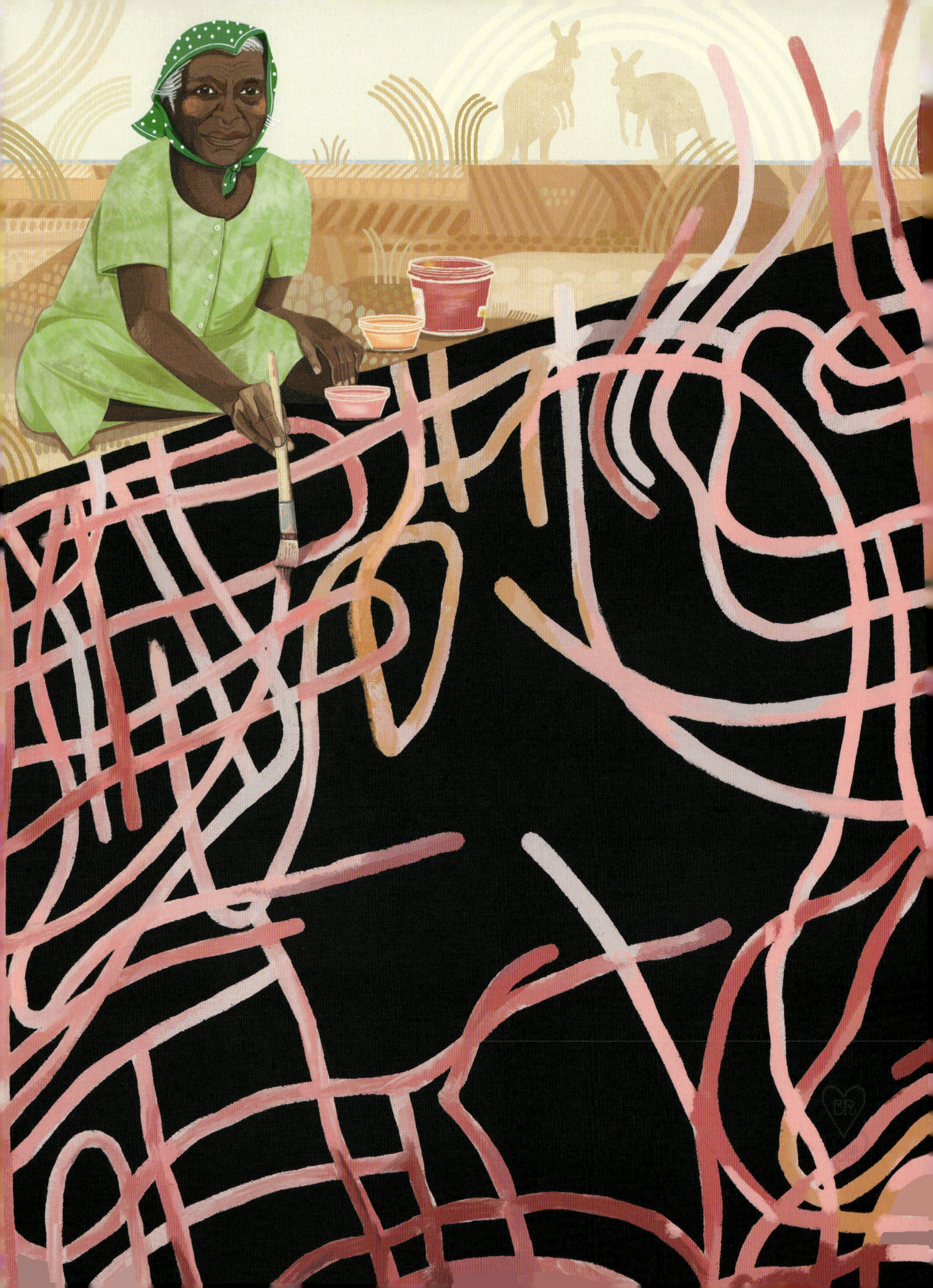

Emily Kame Kngwarreye

Date of Birth: 1910 (approximate date)

Place of Birth: Alhalkere, Utopia, Northern Territory, Australia

UTOPIA

Emily was born in Alhalkere country, also known as Utopia. Utopia is a homeland community of Australia's First Nations. Emily's ancestors had cared for the land in the Northern Territories for thousands of years before British colonization. Colonization is when a country or government moves into an area outside its borders and claims it as its own. They gain control of the land by force, taking wealth and resources from the people already living there. Colonization continues to impact people worldwide today.

THE STOLEN GENERATION

Emily was the youngest of three siblings. She didn't have any children but cared for her niece Barbara Weir. But one day, the government took Barbara away from Emily because of a change in the law known as the Aborigines Protection Act 1909. This change allowed the government to take children from First Nations families and try to make them follow British customs. The children became known as the Stolen Generation. Many years later, Barbara returned to her home and became an artist like her aunt Emily.

BEGINNINGS WITH BATIK

Emily's career as an artist started later in life. At almost seventy, she learned batik through a workshop for women in her community. Batik is a technique where you put hot wax on fabric, dye it different colors, and remove the wax in boiling water. Emily and other artists in her community started the Utopia Women's Batik Group. Over time, the artists learned different techniques, used new materials, and created unique art styles.

PROLIFIC PAINTER

In 1988, Emily began painting on canvas with acrylic. For the next eight years, she made more than three thousand paintings. That is about one every day! She would lay a large canvas on the ground and paint while sitting on the floor. Sometimes dogs and other animals would walk across her work. Looking closely, you can sometimes see paw prints in the paint!

A WHOLE LOT

Emily was an established Anmatyerre elder deeply connected to her homeland community and traditions. The Anmatyerre are indigenous Australian people from the Northern Territory. Her use of colors, lines, and shapes embodied her surroundings and everything about her. Emily's art was a mixture of many things, and she described her art as being a "whole lot."

FAST FACT
She created almost three thousand paintings in eight years.

Batik Painting

Create a design on fabric using a batik technique.

MATERIALS

- Muslin or white cotton fabric
- Cardboard
- Masking tape
- Washable white liquid glue
- Acrylic paint
- Paint palette
- Paintbrushes
- Water cups

VOCABULARY

BATIK: A technique where an artist applies a design onto cloth using a removable substance such as wax. After the fabric is dyed, the wax is removed, revealing the design.

RESIST: To prevent or stop something from happening.

WASH: A thin layer of paint.

ART CONNECTIONS

Batik is an art form that has existed for thousands of years throughout Asia, Africa, and the Middle East. The technique involves covering areas of cloth with a removable substance such as wax. The fabric is dyed, and the wax is removed in hot water. Once dried, the wax designs appear in the fabric's original color. In her first batik paintings, Emily used many fine lines, details, and dots. She would use natural color dyes such as red and yellow ochre. But over time, Emily's style evolved, and by the 1990s, she began using wide marks and a variety of bright colors.

Fig. 1: Cut a piece of fabric and cardboard.

Fig. 2: Tape the fabric onto the cardboard.

Fig. 3: Draw a design with liquid glue.

Let's Get Started!

1: Cut a sheet of fabric. **Fig. 1**

You can cut it into any size and shape. For my example, I cut a 9" × 10" (23 × 25.5 cm) rectangle.

2: Cut a piece of cardboard slightly larger than your fabric. **Fig. 1**

3: Tape the fabric along all sides onto the cardboard. **Fig. 2**

4: Although traditional batik uses hot wax as a **resist**, we can use liquid glue to achieve a similar result. Draw a design using liquid glue. Like Emily, find inspiration in your surroundings. Feel free to experiment using different lines and shapes.

Once done, let the glue dry for a few hours or overnight. **Fig. 3**

5: Mix acrylic paint with water in a cup. Apply a thin **wash** of paint over your design. You can add more than one paint wash to make the colors brighter. **Fig. 4**

6: After the paint is dry, remove the fabric from the cardboard. Use warm water to wash away the glue. You may need to use your fingernails to peel away some of the glue. **Fig. 5**

7: Place your fabric somewhere to dry. You can tie a string and use pins to hang it outside or place it on a drying rack inside. **Fig. 6**

Fig. 4: Apply thin washes of acrylic paint.

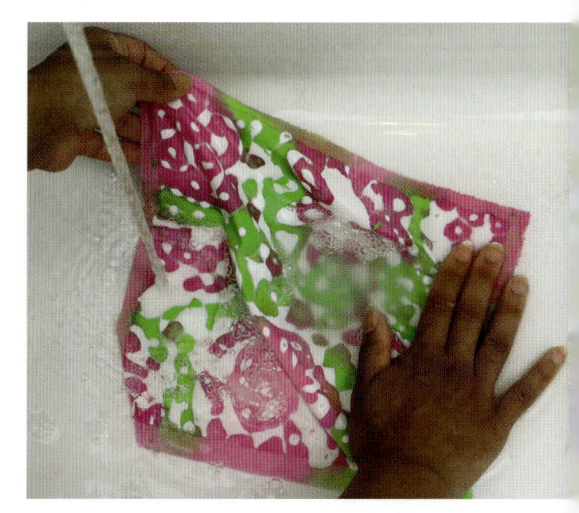

Fig. 5: Use warm water to wash and peel the glue away.

Fig. 6: Hang your fabric to dry.

TECHNIQUES & TIPS

- Try creating multiple layers of colored designs! Apply a simple design to your fabric before adding a layer of paint. Before washing away the glue, apply another design and coat of paint. Your second design will now be in the first color that you applied. You can repeat these steps to create many layers of color.

- Today, many artists experiment using various resist methods, materials, and surfaces. Their designs range from intricate patterns to abstract compositions. Instead of just painting or dyeing the fabric, experiment with splashing or stenciling on colors.

- Batik is a resist technique. Another resist technique you can try at home uses watercolor and crayons. Draw or write on a sheet of paper using a white crayon and apply a wash of watercolor paint on top. Notice how the design you drew in crayon emerges from the page! Because the crayon is wax-based, it resists the watercolor.

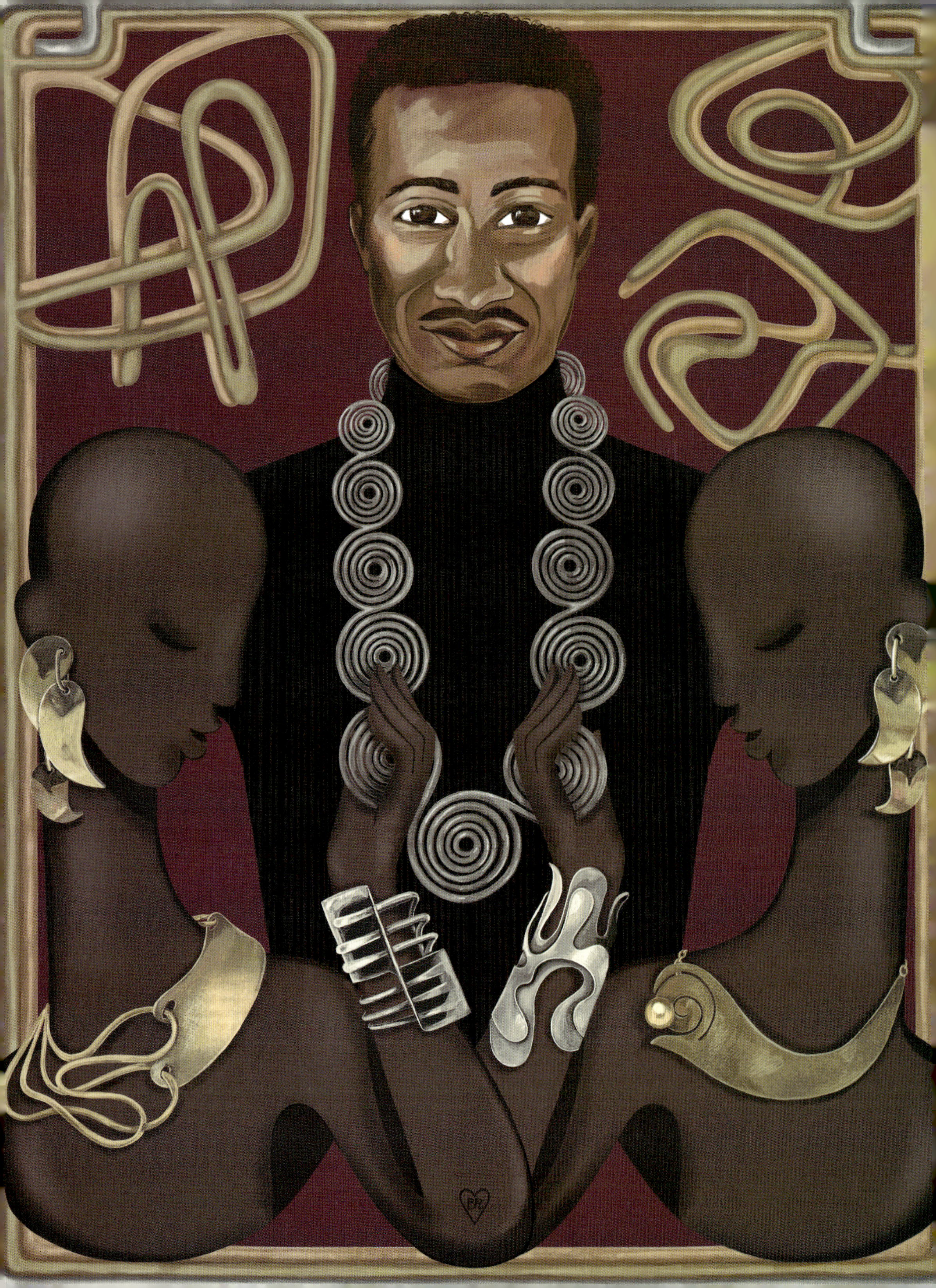

Arthur George Smith

Date of Birth: October 28, 1917

Place of Birth: Cuba

ART STUDENT

In 1914, Arthur's parents and sister migrated from Jamaica to Cuba. After Arthur was born, the family soon moved to New York City. At school, Arthur excelled in the arts, and he won an award for a poster contest. His teachers encouraged Arthur to apply to art schools, and he was offered a full scholarship to Cooper Union, a well-known college in Manhattan.

EARLY CAREER

Arthur graduated college and got a job painting signs for the YMCA. He also started teaching art at the Children's Aid Society. That's where he met Winifred Mason, a jewelry artist. Arthur was so interested in what she did that he started making things with metal. Later, when Winifred opened a store, she hired Arthur as her assistant and taught him how to make jewelry.

ARTSMITH JEWELRY

After some time, an investor suggested that Arthur start his own business. He gave Arthur money to open his first store called ArtSmith Jewelry near Little Italy in New York City. However, because of racism and homophobia, neighbors threatened Arthur and damaged his store. Fearing for his safety, Arthur eventually moved to nearby Greenwich Village.

LEADING MODERNIST JEWELER

When Arthur moved to Greenwich Village, he found a welcoming LGBTQ+ community. He met other artists like him, including a dancer named Talley Beatty. Arthur started making large jewelry pieces for Talley's dance shows, and his work became well known. Arthur also began selling his silver, brass, and copper jewelry in stores throughout the US. People loved Arthur's jewelry, and magazines like *Vogue* and *Harper's Bazaar* featured his work.

Arthur also began making custom designs for people. Some famous pieces include a brooch for Eleanor Roosevelt and cufflinks for Duke Ellington. In 1969, he exhibited his art at the Museum of Contemporary Crafts, now called the Museum of Arts and Design.

LAST PIECE

Arthur was a passionate advocate for the rights of African Americans and the LGBTQ+ community, and he reflected that in his art. He incorporated colors and symbols to express his support in many of his pieces. By the 1960s, the civil rights movement was taking place across the US, and Greenwich Village became a center for the gay rights movement.

Sadly, Arthur got very sick with a heart condition and had to close his store in the late 1970s. He made one last outstanding piece of jewelry, called the *Last Necklace*, before passing away in Brooklyn.

FAST FACT

He was an activist for African American and gay rights.

Wearable Art

Construct a wearable art piece.

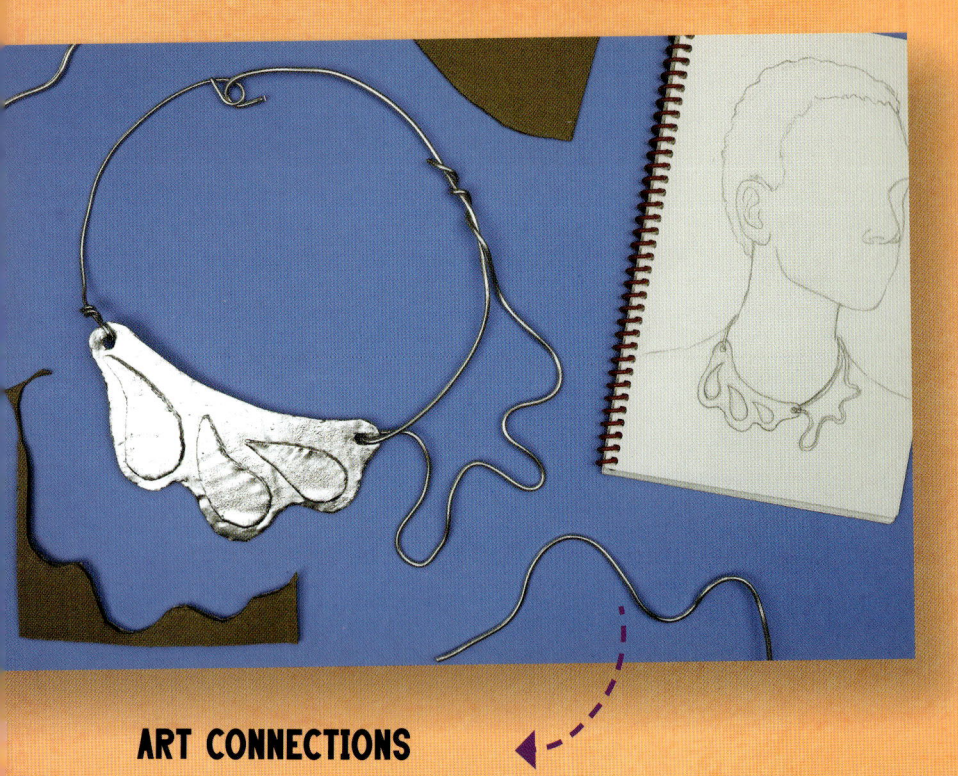

MATERIALS
- Paper
- Pencil
- Cardboard
- Scissors
- Wire
- White glue
- Hole puncher (optional)
- Pliers (optional)
- Metallic acrylic paint
- Paintbrushes
- Paint palette

ART CONNECTIONS

Arthur referred to his jewelry as wearable art and felt that the body was an essential part of the design. He was very thoughtful about how to wear the jewelry and created many sketches before construction. Arthur said, "Like line, form, and color, the body is a material to work with." In addition to the human body, Arthur often used **biomorphic** forms in his work. Biomorphic forms are the organic shapes and patterns we see in nature and living things. Artists have used biomorphic forms in paintings, industrial designs, and architecture. One example is the Sagrada Familia church by Antoni Gaudí. The entire building is inspired by nature. When you look inside, you can see the columns resembling trees and branches filled with leaves reaching toward the ceiling.

VOCABULARY

BIOMORPHIC: Forms that come from the organic shapes and patterns in nature and living things.

EMBELLISHMENT: A decorative detail added to something to make it more beautiful.

GAUGE: How thick or thin a wire is.

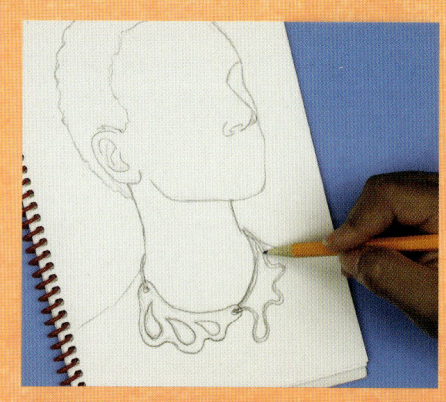

Fig. 1: Sketch a design for a wearable necklace sculpture.

Fig. 2: Cut cardboard to construct the embellishments for your necklace.

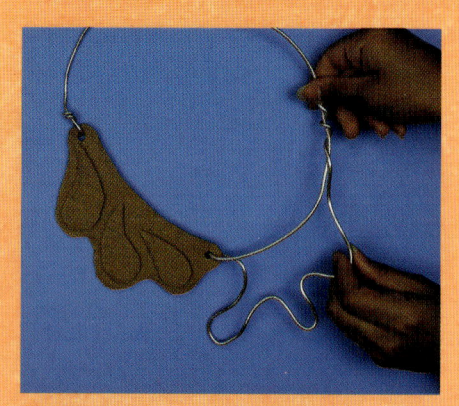

Fig. 3: Use wire to attach the embellishments.

Let's Get Started!

1: The human body was an important part of Arthur's wearable art. For this activity, we will create a necklace. Begin by drawing a head, neck, and shoulders.

2: Imagine how you want the necklace to look and move while wearing it. Like Arthur, find inspiration from your life and use biomorphic lines and forms to sketch a unique design. **Fig. 1**

3: Arthur used metal sheets to fabricate his work, but you can use cardboard instead. Begin by constructing the flat **embellishments** of your necklace. If making more than one embellishment, use wire or glue to attach the pieces. **Fig. 2**

4: Attach the embellishments using two long pieces of wire. Use a hole puncher or pierce the wire through the cardboard. Use your fingers or pliers to twist the end of the wires to secure the embellishments. **Fig. 3**

5: Make a hook-and-eye clasp to put your necklace on and take it off. To make the clasp, use pliers and bend one end to make a circular loop. Bend the other wire end to make a hook. **Fig. 4**

6: Use metallic paint to cover the cardboard pieces. **Fig. 5**

7: Once the paint has dried, try on your wearable art! Bend the wire to make any needed adjustments. **Fig. 6**

8: Design and create other wearable art pieces. Like Arthur, you can construct bracelets, earrings, brooches, and more!

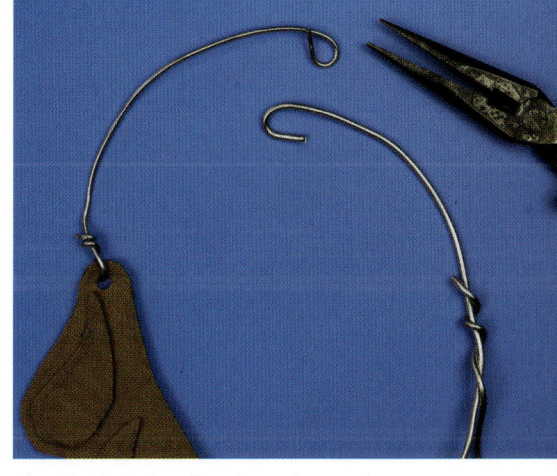

Fig. 4: Create a hook-and-eye clasp.

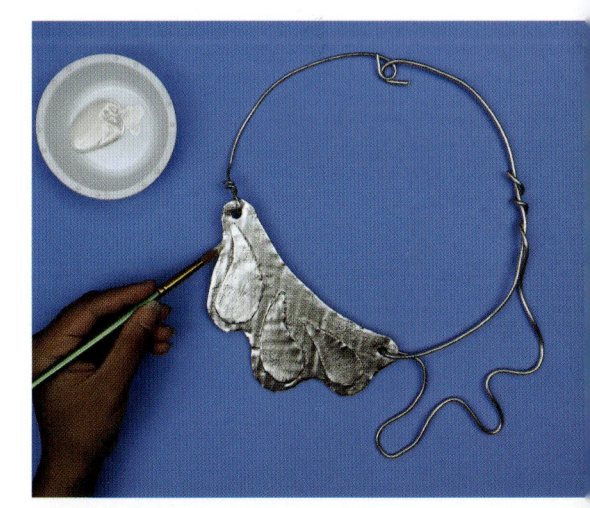

Fig. 5: Cover the cardboard with metallic paint.

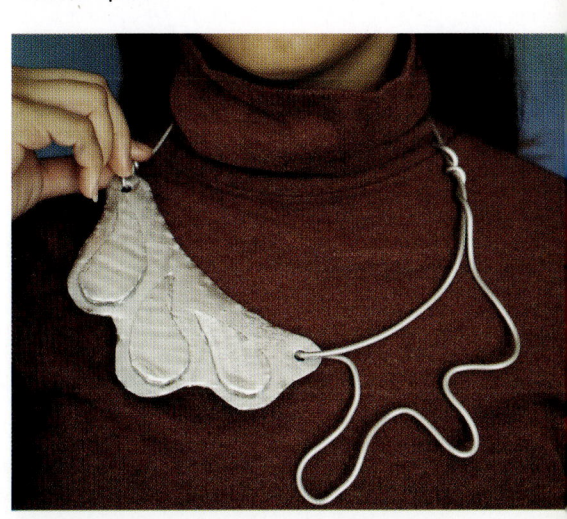

Fig. 6: Wear and adjust your art to your body.

TECHNIQUES & TIPS

- Wire comes in a variety of **gauges**. The gauge refers to how thick or thin the wire is. The higher the gauge number, the thinner the wire. The lower the gauge number, the thicker the wire. Thinner wires are good for small details while thicker wires are better for making links and clasps.

- Wire can also be soft or hard. Softer wires are easier to bend than harder wires. However, harder wires will hold their shape better.

- If you are using a thick or hard wire, you may need to use wire cutters instead of scissors.

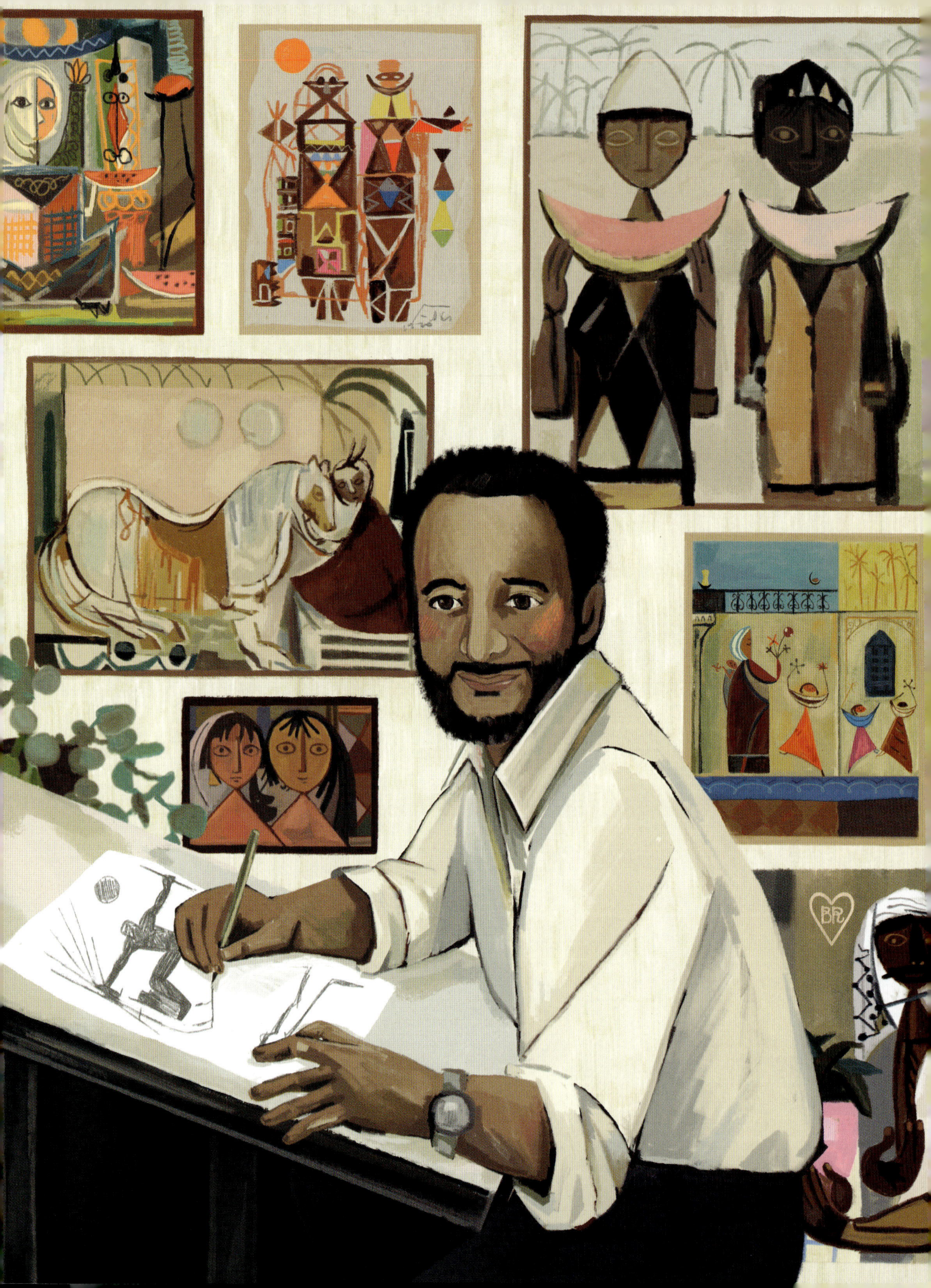

Jewad Selim

Date of Birth: 1919 (approximate date)

Place of Birth: Ankara, present-day Turkey

FAMILY OF ARTISTS

Jewad was born in Ankara, Turkey, to Iraqi parents. When he was a baby, the family moved to Baghdad. Growing up in Iraq, Jewad's family was full of artists. His father was a landscape painter, his mother a talented embroiderer, and his siblings all became artists. In 1938, Jewad got a scholarship to study sculpture in France and Italy. Unfortunately, because of World War II, he had to leave and could not finish his studies.

DISTINCT ARTISTIC STYLE

When he returned to Baghdad, Jewad started working at an archaeology museum. While restoring artifacts, he developed an appreciation of ancient art. He started using these traditional elements and patterns in his own work. After the war was over, Jewad enrolled in the Slade School of Fine Art in London. While there, he met and fell in love with a fellow art student Lorna. They got married in 1950 and moved permanently to Baghdad. Jewad became a teacher and head of the Institute of Fine Arts sculpture department. He encouraged his students to create a unique Iraqi style, and he became an important figure in shaping the modern art movement in Iraq.

BAGHDAD GROUP FOR MODERN ART

In 1951, Jewad founded the Baghdad Modern Art Group. The group wanted to create a distinct Iraqi identity through modern art. Although Iraq was a relatively new country, it has one of the world's oldest and most significant cultural histories. The group wanted to build on this heritage while incorporating local and contemporary culture. Throughout the 1950s, members of the group exhibited worldwide. Artists that were a part of the Baghdad Modern Art Group included Jewad's wife, Lorna, and his brother and sister.

SCULPTOR AND PAINTER

Jewad continued teaching while working on his art at night in a studio he shared with his wife. Even though Jewad was a trained sculptor, he created a series of paintings showing everyday life in Baghdad. These semi-abstract paintings pictured scenes of street vendors, families, and kids playing.

THE MONUMENT OF FREEDOM

In 1959, the government hired Jewad to create a monument remembering the events that led to the creation of Iraq as a country. Sadly, Jewad passed away before the project was complete. He was only forty-two years old, and his death was a sad loss for the art world. His wife helped supervise the rest of the project. They named the completed monument Nasb al-Hurriyah (Freedom Monument), and it can be found in Tahrir Square. Even though some people have tried to destroy it, this national landmark has stayed strong and still stands today.

FAST FACT

He is considered the founder of modern art in Iraq.

Capturing Community

Paint the everyday people in your community.

MATERIALS

- Watercolor paper
- Pencil
- Tempera paint
- Paintbrushes
- Paint palette
- Water cup
- Oil pastels

ART CONNECTIONS

Jewad loved his community and often painted the people and places he saw daily. He also found inspiration in ancient art, including early Islamic manuscript illustrations. These illustrations were unique at the time because they showed everyday life and had expressive faces, bright colors, and decorative patterns. Jewad used similar elements in his paintings. But instead of painting things realistically, he used shapes to simplify things. One shape Jewad used a lot in his works is the **crescent**. The crescent symbolizes the cradle of civilization and represents the source of life in the Middle Eastern region. Like Jewad, you can find inspiration in the things around you by looking at the people, patterns, and shapes that make your community unique.

VOCABULARY

CRESCENT: A semicircular shape that tapers to a point at each end.

SEMI-ABSTRACT: A highly stylized design that remains somewhat recognizable.

PASTEL: Any light or pale color that has low saturation.

Fig. 1: Draw a place in your community.

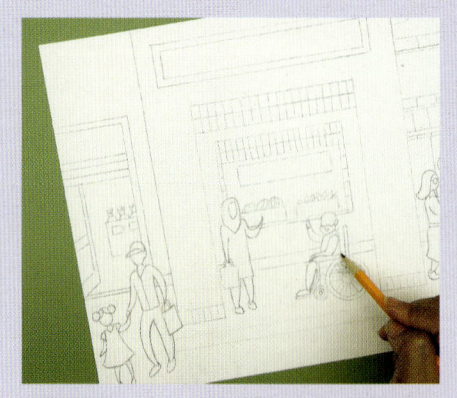

Fig. 2: Draw the people in your community.

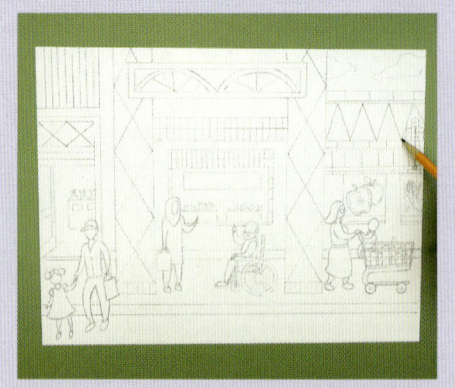

Fig. 3: Complete your drawing.

76 BE A CREATIVE CHANGEMAKER: A KIDS' ART ACTIVITY BOOK

Let's Get Started!

1: Many of Jewad's paintings show everyday life in Baghdad. Find inspiration in your local community. Think of the people and places you see daily. This could be the cashier at your local market, your neighbors walking their dogs, or your classmates playing at the park.

2: Use a pencil to draw one of the places you like to visit in your community. Like Jewad, keep your drawing **semi-abstract**. That means it does not need to be realistic but should still be recognizable. **Fig. 1**

3: Within your drawing, add two or more people from your community. Consider what they are doing and how they are interacting with each other. **Fig. 2**

4: Complete your drawing by adding additional people and details you see in your community. Use geometric shapes and patterns to adorn any empty space. **Fig. 3**

5: Use tempera paint to add color to your work. Use a large brush to paint the big areas in the background first. Consider using a **pastel** color palette similar to Jewad's. **Fig. 4**

6: Use a small brush to paint the remaining areas and people. **Fig. 5**

7: Once your painting is dry, use oil pastels to add any lines, patterns, or details. **Fig. 6**

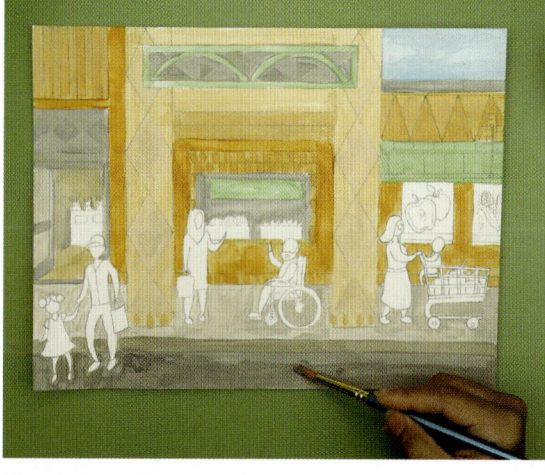

Fig. 4: Paint large areas.

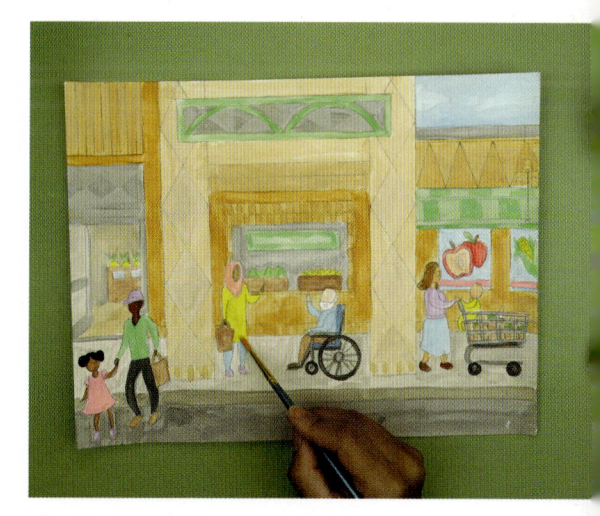

Fig. 5: Complete your painting.

Fig. 6: Add final details.

TECHNIQUES & TIPS

- Try using geometric shapes to draw people. Draw an oval for the head, a triangle for the neck, a rectangle for the body, and crescents for the arms.

- Jewad's palette included pastel and earth tones such as light yellows, soft blues, and pale greens. Consider using similar colors in your painting by adding white to any color to make it pastel.

JEWAD SELIM

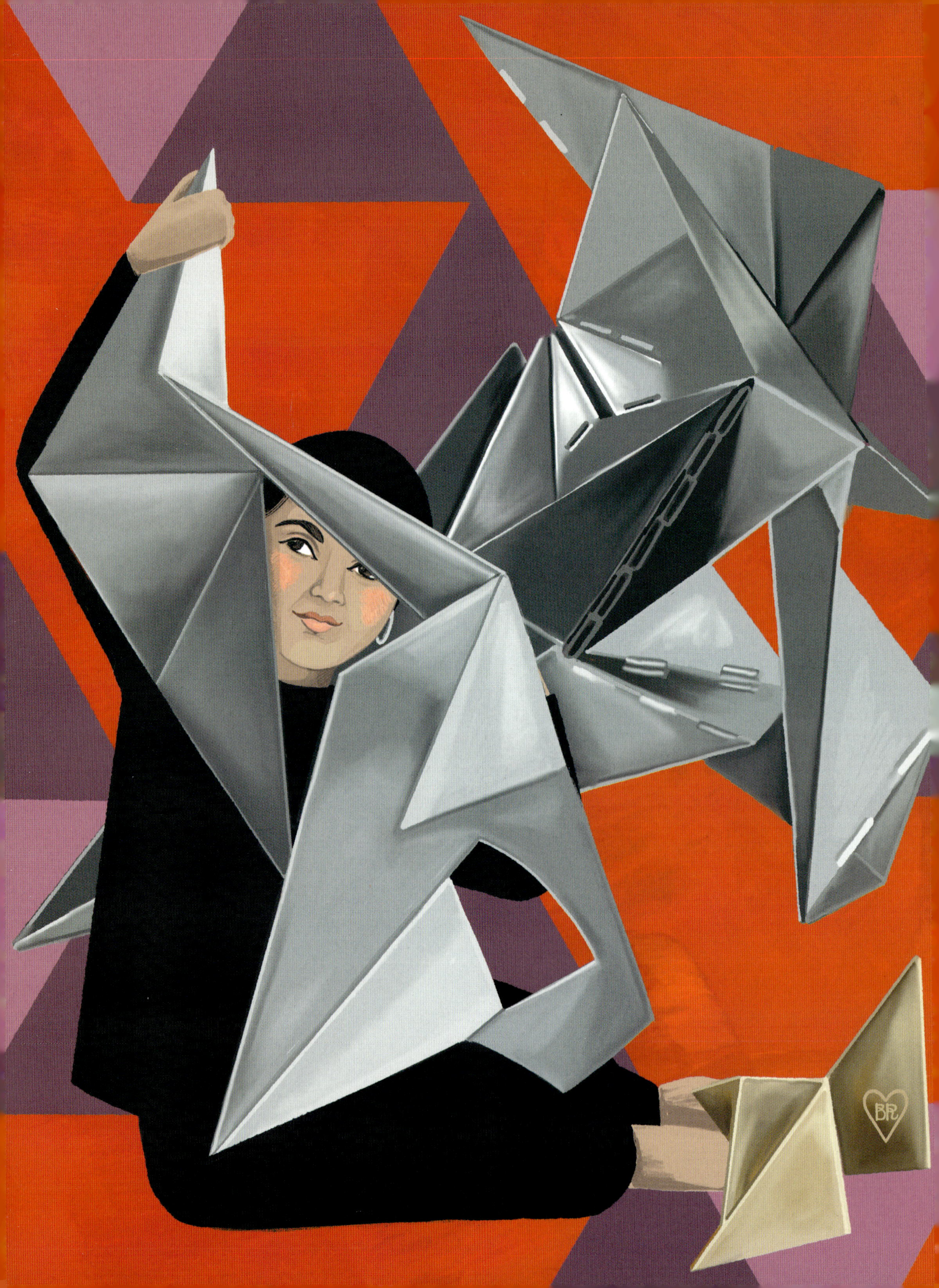

Lygia Clark

Date of Birth: October 23, 1920

Place of Birth: Belo Horizonte, Brazil

AN OUTSIDER

Lygia Pimentel Lins was born in Belo Horizonte, one of the largest cities in Brazil. She described her childhood as hard and felt like an outsider in her family. Lygia was married at eighteen and moved to Rio de Janeiro. After her third child was born, she started taking art classes with modernists Roberto Burle Marx and Zélia Ferreira Salgado.

PARIS PAINTINGS

Lygia was talented, and her husband and friends encouraged her to go to Paris to study painting. In 1950, Lygia moved to Paris with her children and studied with other abstract artists. There she made a series of geometric oil paintings, charcoal portraits of her kids, and pictures of staircases. After two years in Paris, the family moved back to Rio de Janeiro. Not long after, Lygia divorced but continued to use the surname Clark.

VENICE BIENNALE

Lygia won many awards and showed her art throughout Brazil. In 1954, she was selected to represent Brazil in an international art exhibition called the Venice Biennale. This exhibition takes place in Italy and is one of the world's most important art events. Lygia exhibited her art at the Venice Biennale four times.

THE ORGANIC LINE

She also came up with a new idea called "the organic line," which is the space between the frame and the canvas in a painting. Lygia described this space as a connection between art and life. She also applied this idea to architecture and saw that the organic line exists all around. She believed that architects and artists should use the organic line to rethink how we see the spaces and objects around us, such as doors, windows, and tiles on the floor.

ART AS EXPERIENCE

Lygia began to explore the relationship between inside and outside, between oneself and the world. She moved from painting to sculpture and discovered new ways for people to interact with her artwork. One of her most well-known series is titled *Bichos*, which means "critters" when translated from Portuguese. These *Bichos* were aluminum sculptures with hinges that allowed people to move the pieces. Lygia referred to these hinges as backbones and felt that the *Bichos* were living. The sculpture itself was not art. It was the experience of moving and interacting with the piece that she considered to be art.

She continued exploring this concept of art as a lived experience. Lygia began to organize what she called "participatory propositions." During these events, participants would wear art objects such as soft masks and mirrored goggles. Each interaction was a unique moment as art. Lygia also believed that art had the power to transform and heal, later becoming a leader of art therapy.

FAST FACT

She explored the relationship between herself and the world.

Interactive Sculptures

Construct an interactive and movable sculpture.

MATERIALS
- Cardboard
- Pencil
- Ruler
- Scissors
- Masking tape
- Tempera or acrylic paint
- Paintbrushes
- Paint palette
- Water cup

VOCABULARY

BICHOS: Portuguese word for "critters."

INTERACTIVE: Responding to and acting upon one another.

HINGE: A joint or flexible piece that allows movement.

ART CONNECTIONS

Lygia Clark's *Bichos* are foldable sculptures meant to be **interacted** with and rearranged by the viewer. Each piece consists of many geometric aluminum pieces connected through **hinges**. The sculptures can open, close, fold, and turn. Because there is no "right" way to display them, there is no front or back, inside or outside. They were created as a series and range in size, from small *Bichos* that fit in your hands to larger-than-life *Bichos* that fill entire rooms. Lygia made about seventy *Bichos*, each challenging how we look at and interact with art.

Fig. 1: Draw diagonal lines across a piece of cardboard.

Fig. 2: Cut and trim the cardboard pieces.

Fig. 3: Tape two cardboard pieces together.

Let's Get Started!

1: Find a rectangular piece of cardboard. Draw two diagonal lines from top to bottom. Draw two more diagonal lines from left to right. You should now have nine geometric shapes drawn. **Fig. 1**

2: Cut along the lines. Trim some of the shapes to create triangles and semicircles. **Fig. 2**

3: Lygia Clark's *Bichos* used pins to create metal hinges, but we can use tape instead. Select two cardboard pieces to tape together. Make sure that the edges you are attaching are the same length. Apply tape to both the front and back. **Fig. 3**

4: Tape the remaining cardboard pieces together. Arrange and trim your sculpture as you work to make sure it can easily move. **Fig. 4**

5: Lay your sculpture flat and paint the entire surface. **Fig. 5**

6: Once the paint has dried, flip your sculpture over and paint the other side. **Fig. 5**

7: After the paint has dried, arrange your sculpture. Invite others to interact with your artwork! **Fig. 6**

Fig. 4: Tape the remaining cardboard pieces together.

Fig. 5: Paint your sculpture.

Fig. 6: Arrange your sculpture and invite others to interact with it!

TECHNIQUES & TIPS

- Leave a small space between your cardboard pieces when taping the hinge. This will give the cardboard more space to move and bend.

- Lygia's *Bichos* sculptures were made from aluminum. Instead of paint, you can wrap your sculpture in aluminum foil. Use glue to secure the edges of the foil onto the cardboard.

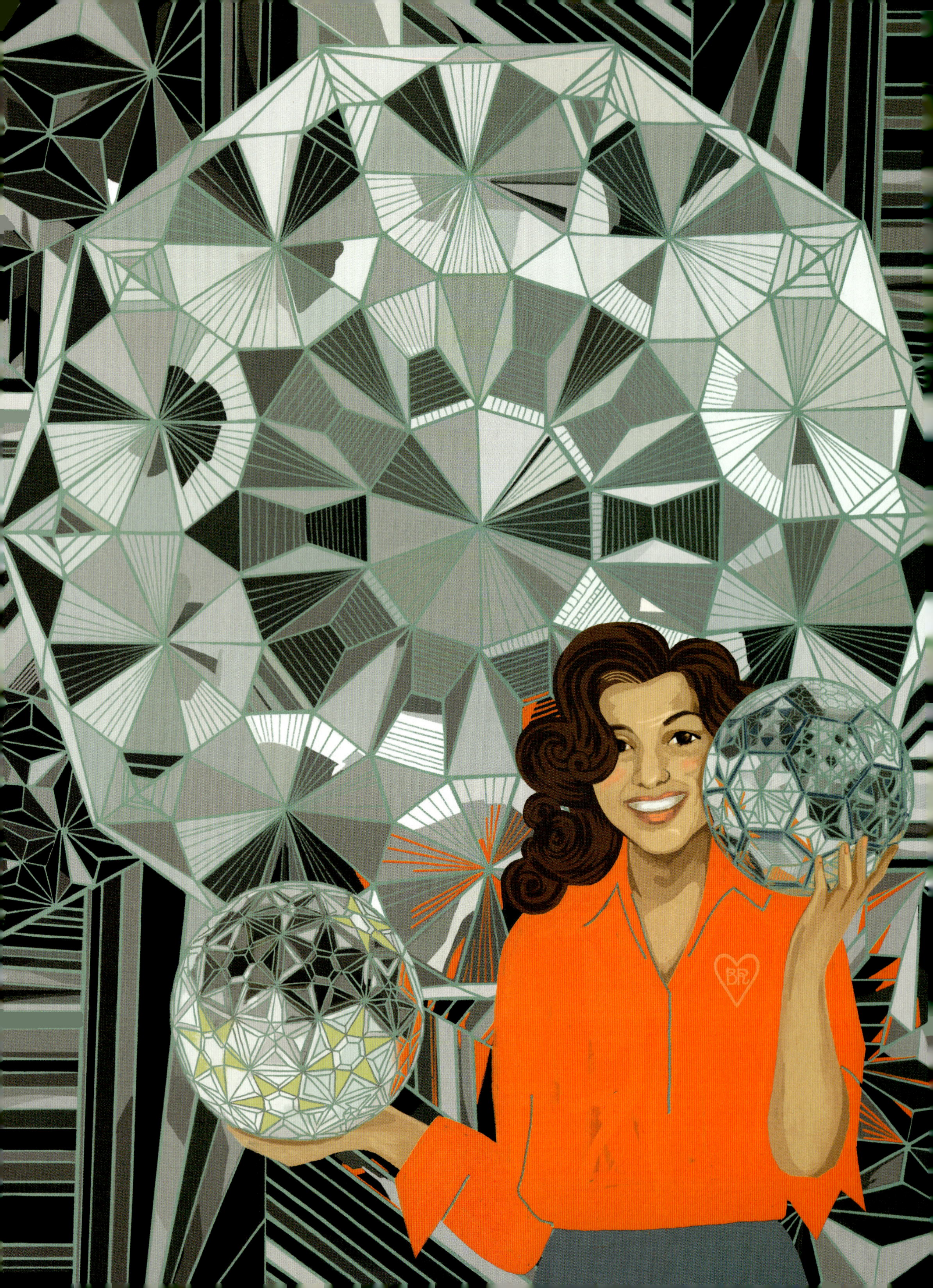

Monir Shahroudy Farmanfarmaian

Date of Birth: December 16, 1922

Place of Birth: Qazvin, present-day Iran

IRANIAN ANCESTRY

Monir was born in a city called Qazvin in Iran. Her family had a long history of important people like religious leaders, traders, and Ottoman aristocracy. Her childhood home was filled with paintings, stained-glass windows, and gardens, which later inspired her art. When she was a child, her father became a member of parliament, and they moved to the capital city of Tehran. There she started taking art lessons and learned to draw by copying pictures on postcards. She wanted to become an artist and went to university for a semester before moving to New York City in 1945.

MOVE TO NEW YORK

Monir studied fashion illustration at Parsons School of Design in New York. She became a freelance artist who drew clothes and textile designs for magazines such as *Vogue* and created fashion layouts for stores. Even though she became successful as an artist in the US, she moved back to Iran in 1957.

FLORAL MONOTYPES

Upon returning to Tehran, Monir married a young lawyer. She set up a rooftop studio and began experimenting with monotype printing. A monotype is a form of printmaking where the artist paints on a smooth surface and transfers the image onto paper. Monotypes are unique because only one print is made instead of many. Monir loved gardening, so she included flowers in her work. By 1963 she had her first solo show of over one hundred floral monotypes.

MIRROR MOSAICS

In the early 1960s, Monir visited a mosque called Shāh Chérāgh, which is Persian for "King of the Light." The walls and ceiling are covered with small mirror tiles reflecting light. Monir was fascinated by how the light changed the space and wanted to use similar mirror tiles in her art. Since this was an ancient tradition, Monir hired an expert to teach her how to do it. She used this technique with reverse-glass painting and geometry found in Islamic architecture to create a series of mirror mosaics.

HEARTACHES

After the Iranian Revolution in 1979, Monir quickly moved back to New York City. She didn't know when she would be able to return to Iran, so she set up a studio and continued her work. During this time, she made a series of small box sculptures called *Heartaches*. In the series, Monir expresses her pain and sadness about having to leave Iran abruptly. Monir eventually returned to Tehran and set up her studio again in 2004. She rehired a few old art assistants and trained new ones to help her create her large-scale mirror mosaics. Monir continued to live and work in Tehran until she passed in 2019.

FAST FACT

She combined traditional Persian art techniques with contemporary designs.

Mirror Mosaic

Use radial symmetry to design a mirror mosaic.

MATERIALS

- 8" × 8" (20.5 × 20.5 cm) drawing paper
- Scissors
- Soft lead pencil
- Metal spoon
- Mirror film
- Transparent tape
- Pen
- Permanent markers
- 8" × 8" (20.5 × 20.5 cm) construction paper
- Glue stick

ART CONNECTIONS

The rich cultural history of Persia, now present-day Iran, inspired Monir's art. The mirror **mosaic** technique she used was a traditional Persian process passed down for many generations. Monir also used the principles of Islamic geometry and architecture to create her work. Islamic art often avoids figurative images, and many designs use repeating **geometric shapes** to create detailed patterns. One important shape in Islamic art is the circle because it represents unity and the source of creation. Some artists use a circular pattern that spreads out from the center, known as **radial symmetry**. You can see radial symmetry in several of Monir's mirror mosaics. Over time, Monir experimented with different art techniques and found infinite possibilities in creating.

VOCABULARY

MOSAIC: A pattern or image created by arranging small pieces of material next to each other.

GEOMETRIC SHAPES: Shapes created with a specific amount of lines, points, and curves.

RADIAL SYMMETRY: A form of symmetry where elements are arranged around a circular axis.

Let's Get Started!

1: Cut a sheet of paper into an 8" × 8" (20.5 × 20.5 cm) square. Fold the paper in half vertically, horizontally, and diagonally. Unfold the paper to reveal eight equal triangles. **Fig. 1**

2: Create a geometric radial design. Use a soft lead pencil to draw geometric lines and shapes inside one of the folded triangles. **Fig. 2**

3: Fold your paper in half so the pencil drawing touches the triangle next to it. Use a spoon to rub the back of the drawing, transferring the image onto the other triangle. **Fig. 3**

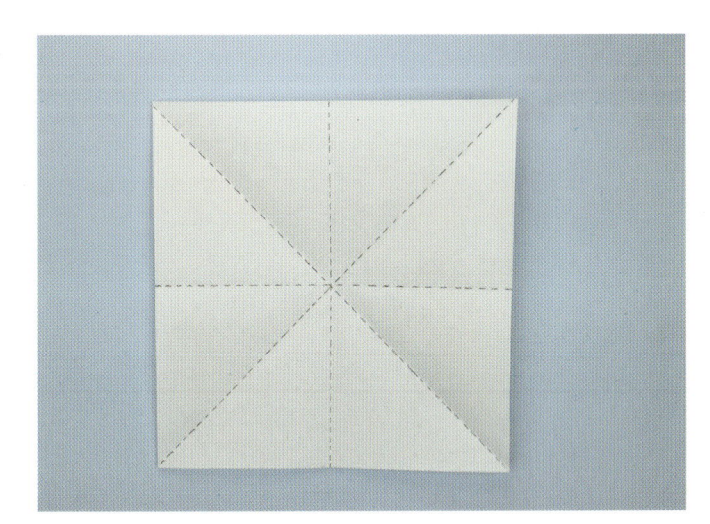

(continued)

Fig. 1: Cut an 8" × 8" (20.5 × 20.5 cm) square and fold it into eighths.

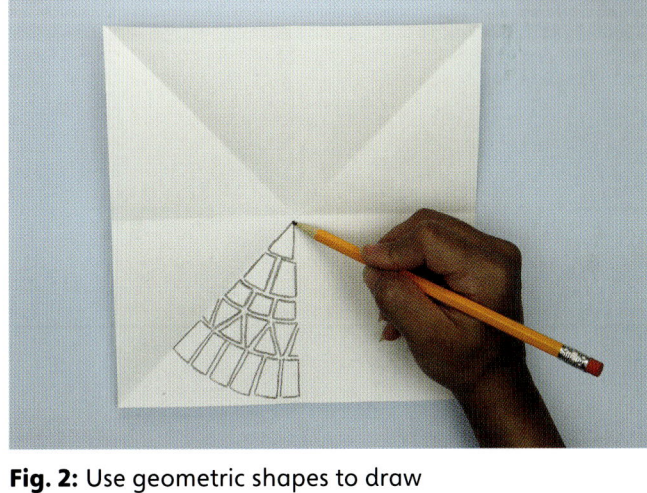

Fig. 2: Use geometric shapes to draw inside one of the triangles.

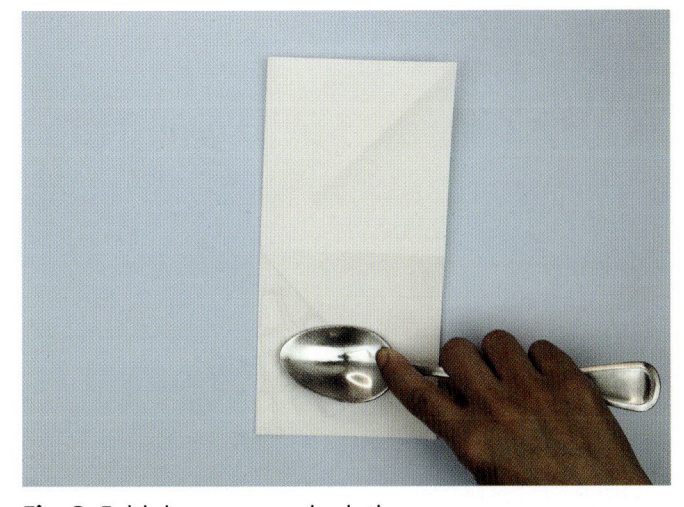

Fig. 3: Fold the paper and rub the back with a spoon to transfer your drawing.

TAKE IT FURTHER!

- Monir did not create work only using radial symmetry. Experiment with making different mosaics using a variety of designs, geometric shapes, and patterns. There are infinite possibilities!

MONIR SHAHROUDY FARMANFARMAIAN

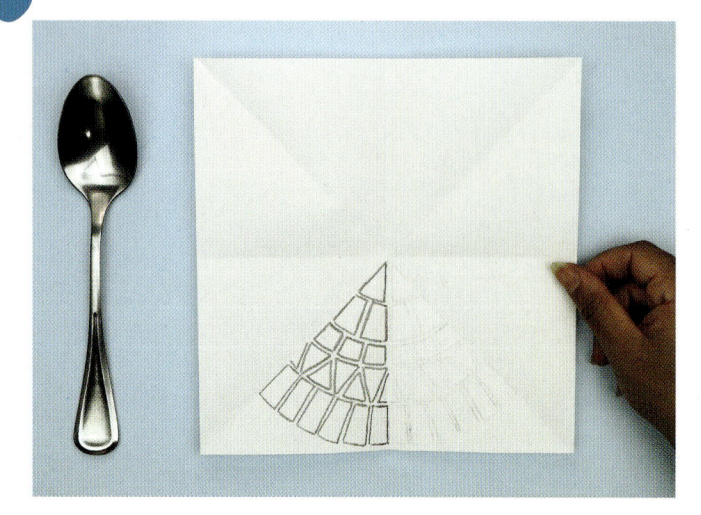

Fig. 4: Unfold to reveal a transfer.

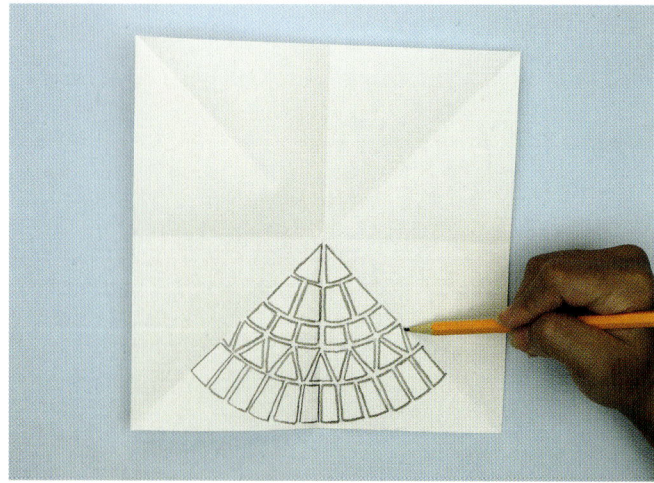

Fig. 5: Trace the transfer.

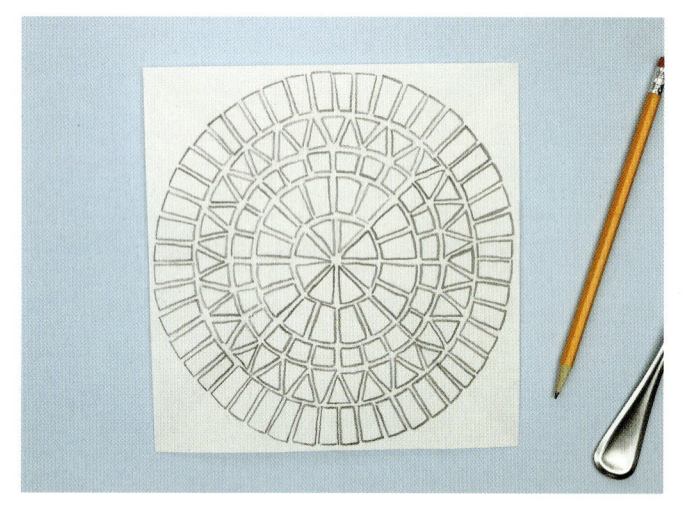

Fig. 6: Repeat the previous steps to complete your radial design.

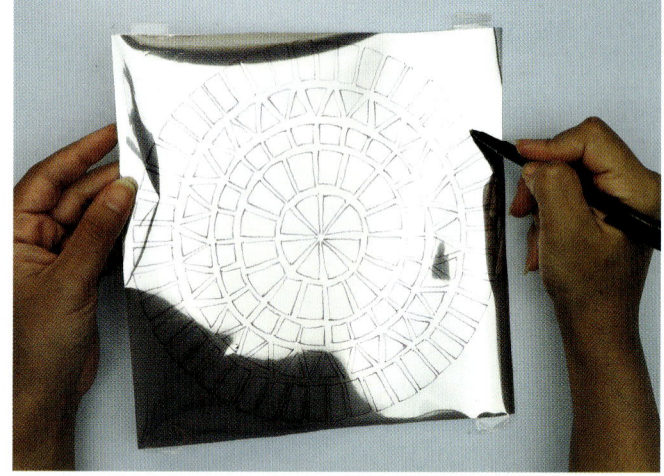

Fig. 7: Tape mirror film on top of the drawing and trace your design.

Fig. 8: Add color to select pieces.

Fig. 9: Cut and arrange your radial design pieces.

86 BE A CREATIVE CHANGEMAKER: A KIDS' ART ACTIVITY BOOK

4: Unfold your paper to see a faint transfer of your drawing. **Fig. 4**

5: Use a soft lead pencil to trace the transfer. **Fig. 5**

6: Repeat steps 3 through 5 to complete your radial design. **Fig. 6**

7: Cutting mirrors is a unique skill that requires specific tools and technical expertise. Instead of actual mirrors, we will use mirror film.

Cut a piece of mirror film to match the size of your paper. Tape it on top of your radial design drawing. Because the material is transparent, you can see your design through the film. Use a pen to trace your design. **Fig. 7**

8: Use permanent markers to add color to select pieces. Consider how you will maintain radial symmetry when adding color. **Fig. 8**

9: Remove the mirror film from your drawing and carefully cut out your radial design pieces. As you cut each piece, arrange them onto construction paper. Leave a small space between each shape. **Fig. 9**

10: Use a glue stick to secure each metallic piece onto the construction paper. **Fig. 10**

11: Cut the excess paper around your design. **Fig. 11**

Fig. 10: Glue your pieces down.

Fig. 11: Cut the excess paper.

TECHNIQUES & TIPS

- Use a soft lead pencil when transferring your drawing from one triangle to another. The number and letter indicate how hard or soft a lead pencil is. A pencil with an *H* is a hard pencil. This lead is harder and will leave lighter marks on the paper. A pencil with a *B* is a soft pencil. This lead is softer and will leave darker marks on the paper. The higher the number before the letter indicates how hard or soft it is. A 4H pencil is harder and lighter than a 2H pencil, whereas a 4B pencil is softer and darker than a 2B pencil.

- If you cannot find mirror film, use aluminum foil instead. Since it is not transparent, you can draw your radial design directly on the foil surface.

- Use color construction paper that complements the colors in your mirror pieces. You can trim your piece into any shape and mount your work onto a different color paper.

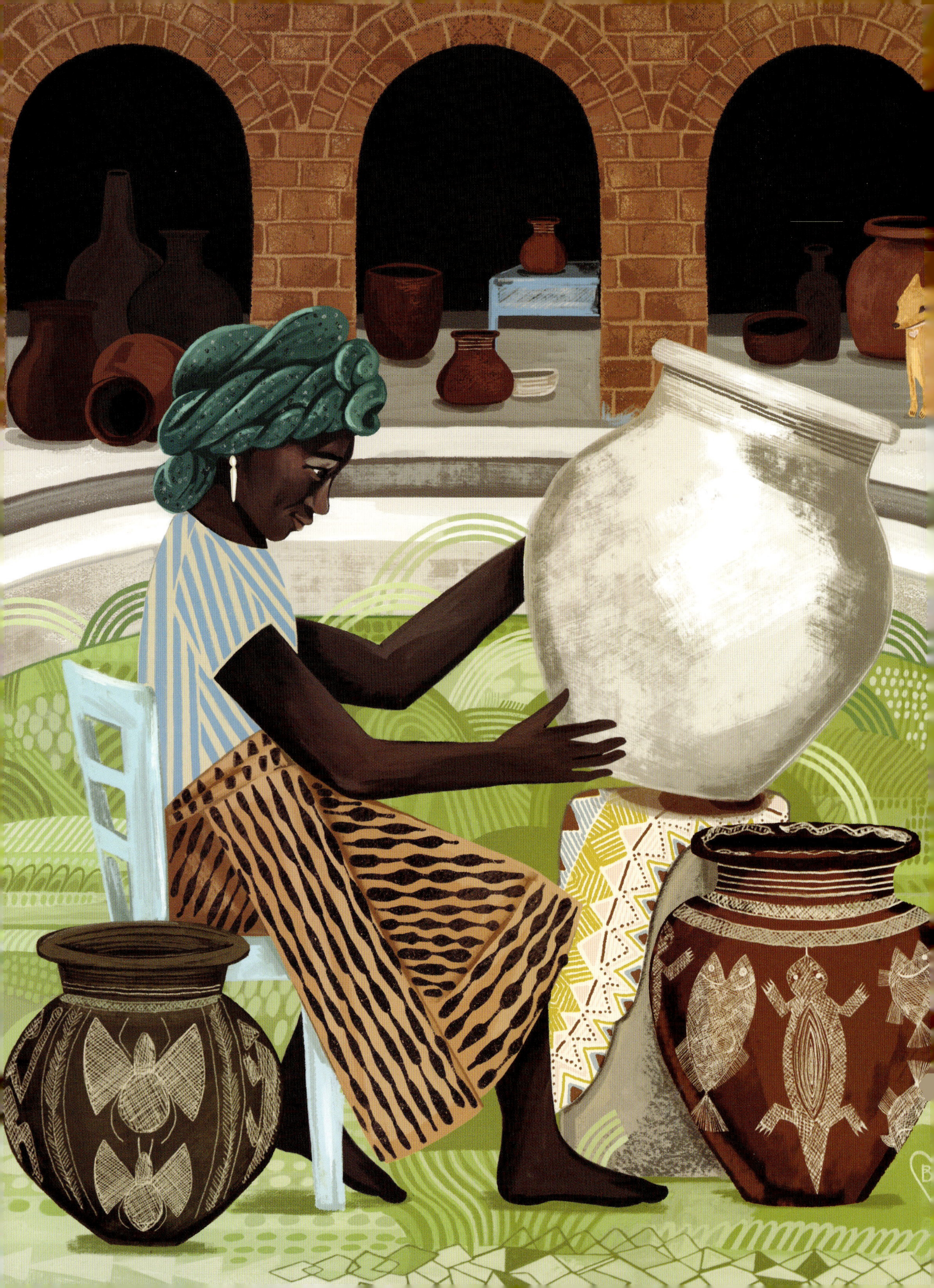

Ladi Kwali

Date of Birth: 1925 (approximate date)

Place of Birth: Kwali, Nigeria

DAUGHTER OF SUNDAY

Ladi was born around 1925 to a family of potters in the Gwari region of Nigeria. Her name Ladi means "Daughter of Sunday," and her last name Kwali is the name of the village where she was born. In this village, pottery is an ancient and important tradition for women. When she was a child, Ladi learned from her aunt how to make pots by hand using techniques such as coiling and pinching. She used these skills to make clay containers such as jars, pots, bowls, and jugs. Her talent was well known, and many families proudly displayed her work in their homes.

ABUJA POTTERY TRAINING CENTER

In 1954, Ladi joined the Abuja Pottery Training Centre, where she learned new techniques such as using a pottery wheel, glazing, and firing in a kiln. She started using these new methods in her work. Ladi was the first female potter at the center, opening the door for more women to join. By 1965, four women opened another pottery workshop nearby called Dakin Gwari.

BREAKING THE MOLD

Even though she had access to modern machinery, Ladi preferred to make most of her pottery by hand. She would take a regular vessel and turn it into a beautiful work of art. She would paint the pottery with a colored slip and use a technique called sgraffito to carve geometric patterns and stylized animals. Her designs included local lizards, snakes, birds, fish, and scorpions. Ladi's art was known for being very detailed and unique.

DISTINGUISHED ARTIST

In the late 1950s and early 1960s, Ladi started showing her work worldwide. She would travel and teach others her skills through lectures and demonstrations. In 1980, Ladi won a significant award in Nigeria called the Nigerian National Order of Merit Award. Even though she traveled the world, she remained a teacher at the Abuja Pottery Training Centre.

IN HER HONOR

After she died, the center was renamed in her honor. Even though the Ladi Kwali Pottery Centre closed in the 1990s, people are trying to open it again. In recognition of her talents, the government printed her portrait on the back of the Nigerian N20 currency note. Ladi's legacy still lives on, and you can find many roads and streets in Nigeria named after her.

FAST FACT
She is the first woman to appear on Nigerian currency.

Sgraffito Pottery

Sculpt a clay vessel and use sgraffito to decorate the surface.

MATERIALS
- Air-dry clay
- Clay tools or fork
- Paintbrushes
- Water
- Butterknife (optional)
- Jar with lid
- Acrylic paint
- Pencil
- Toothpick or other sharp object
- Gloss varnish or sealer

ART CONNECTIONS

Ladi used hand-building techniques she learned from her aunt to sculpt a variety of **vessels**. A vessel is a container used to transport, store, and serve food and drinks. Ceramic vessels include bowls, cups, jars, jugs, pots, and vases. Ladi would then cover these traditional vessels using **sgraffito**. Sgraffito is a technique used for decorating ceramics. After a piece is sculpted, it is dipped into a colored **slip**. A design is then carved through the slip, revealing the color of the clay underneath. Ladi coated her pieces in a dark slip and used a porcupine quill to create the intricate details in her designs.

VOCABULARY

VESSEL: A container used to transport or store something.

SGRAFFITO: A technique where a design is carved through a colored slip to reveal the clay underneath.

SLIP: A liquid mixture of clay and water.

Let's Get Started!

1: Begin with a pinch pot. Roll a piece of clay into a ball. Place it onto a flat surface and push your thumb down into the center. **Fig. 1**

2: Gently pinch the clay between your thumb and fingers. Continue turning and pinching the clay until you have made a bowl shape. This is also known as a pinch pot. Smooth the inside and outside. **Fig. 2**

3: Add height to your vessel using the coiling technique. Roll a piece of clay into a long coil. Ensure the coil is long enough to wrap around the top of your pinch pot. **Fig. 3**

4: Score both pieces to attach the coil to the pinch pot. Use a clay tool or fork to scratch the top surface of your pinch pot and coil. **Fig. 4**

(continued)

Fig. 1: Roll a piece of clay into a ball and push your thumb into the center.

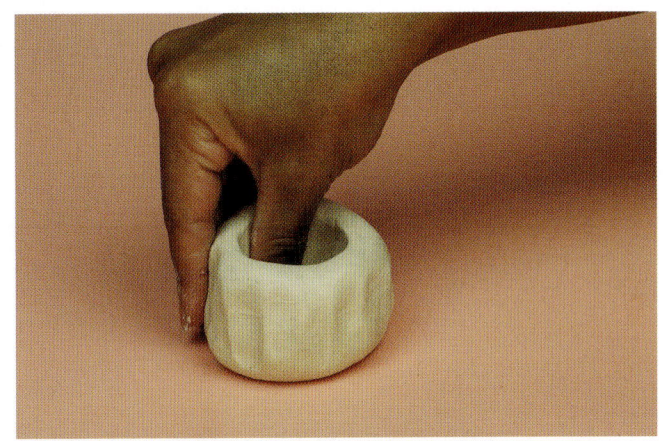

Fig. 2: Pinch and turn the edges of the clay to create a pinch pot.

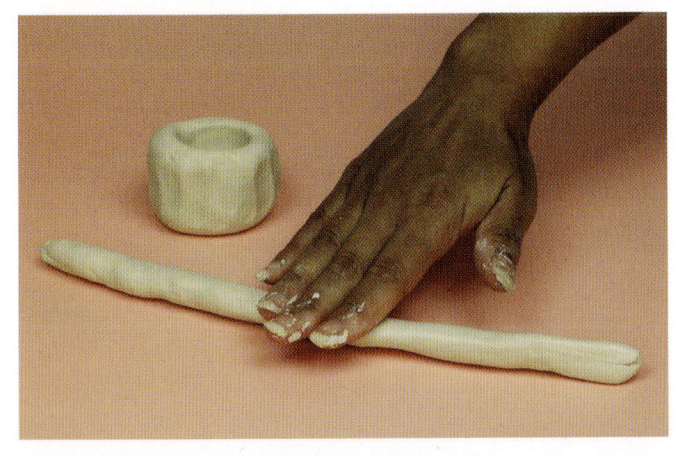

Fig. 3: Roll a piece of clay into a long coil.

Fig. 4: Score the top of your pinch pot and coil.

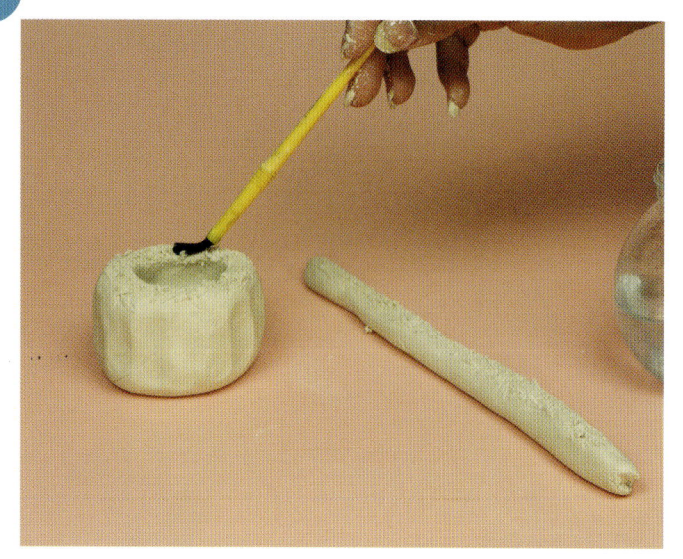

Fig. 5: Add water to the top of your pinch pot and coil.

Fig. 6: Wrap the coil around the top of the pinch pot.

Fig. 7: Smooth the inside and outside.

Fig. 8: Finish building your vessel.

Fig. 9: Make a clay slip.

Fig. 10: Mix and add color to the slip.

5: Use a small paintbrush or your finger to add water on top of the scratched surfaces. **Fig. 5**

6: With the scratched surfaces touching, wrap the coil around the top of the pinch pot. Use a clay tool or butterknife to cut the excess coil. **Fig. 6**

7: Use your finger to smooth the inside and outside of the pot. **Fig. 7**

8: Consider what type of ceramic vessel you want to create. You may sculpt a bowl, cup, jar, jug, pot, vase, or other container. Repeat steps 3 through 7 to build your desired vessel. Allow your pottery to dry overnight. **Fig. 8**

9: After you build your vessel, you will need to create a **slip** to use the next day. Break any remaining clay into small marble-size pieces and place them inside a jar. Add water to the container and seal the lid. Allow the clay to soak in the water overnight while your clay vessel is drying. **Fig. 9**

10: The next day, blend or stir the slip mixture together until it is smooth. Add small amounts of acrylic paint to the slip, stirring it until it is even in color and texture. **Fig. 10**

11: Use a thick brush to apply an even layer of slip all over your dried ceramic vessel. You can add multiple layers of slip to achieve a more vibrant color. **Fig. 11**

12: Once the slip is slightly dried, use a pencil to draw a design. Like Ladi, you may choose to draw geometric patterns and stylized animals. Use a toothpick or another sharp pointed object to carve out the design. Press firmly to remove the slip layer and reveal the clay color beneath. **Fig. 12**

13: Dust off any tiny flecks of colored slip. Use a large, clean brush to apply a clear gloss varnish or sealer. **Fig. 13**

Fig. 11: Cover your clay vessel in a colored slip.

Fig. 12: Carve your design.

Fig. 13: Coat with a clear gloss.

TECHNIQUES & TIPS

- Instead of clay tools, you can use other materials you might find at home. You can use a fork to score and scratch your clay surface, a butterknife to cut your clay coils, and a toothpick to draw your sgraffito design.

- The slip should have a similar consistency to smooth peanut butter. If your slip is too runny, pour out some water and add more clay pieces. Do this before adding any color or acrylic paint to your mixture.

- If your air-dry clay is light in color, consider using a dark color for your slip overcoat. If your air-dry clay is dark in color, consider using a light color for your slip overcoat. By using contrasting colors, your design will be more visible.

- When carving your design, you may need to go over it more than once to remove the outer layer of the slip.

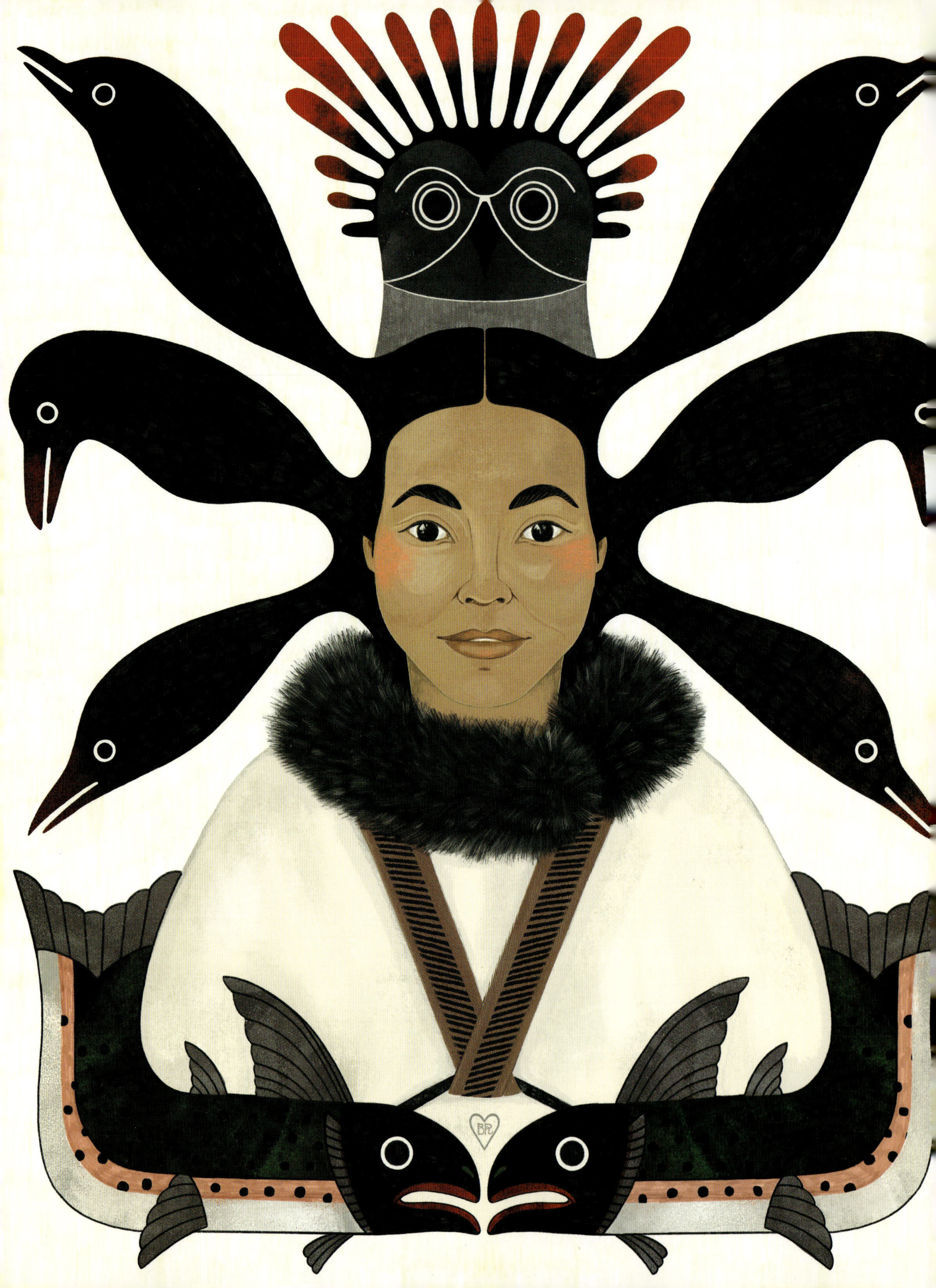
BR

Kenojuak Ashevak

Date of Birth: October 3, 1927

Place of Birth: Ikirasaqa, Baffin Island, Northwest Territories, Canada

SIMPLE BEGINNINGS

Kenojuak was born in Ikirasaqa, an Inuit camp in northwest Canada. Her family followed a nomadic hunting lifestyle. They would travel between different camps in the area in search of food. Art supplies were limited, but she learned how to sew and make clothes from her grandmother. She and her husband, Johnniebo, would also draw using pencils and paper.

RABBIT EATING SEAWEED

In 1952, Kenojuak was diagnosed with tuberculosis and spent three years in the hospital. After she recovered, she started working for an arts program in Cape Dorset, Canada, where she made things like sealskin boots, handbags, and dolls. Her unique designs caught the attention of one of the program's organizers, who encouraged her to turn her drawings into prints. One of Kenojuak's first prints was of a rabbit eating seaweed, which she made by cutting a stencil into sealskin. In 1959, Kenojuak's work first appeared in an art catalog.

WEST BAFFIN COOPERATIVE

Many people in Cape Dorset began making drawings and prints, and the area became a well-known art community. In 1959, Kenojuak was one of the first members of the West Baffin Cooperative. In this group, artists worked together to make art. Kenojuak would draw designs onto smooth slabs of stone before another artist would chisel away around the drawing. Ink would then be rolled onto the raised surface to make many copies. When the print was complete, they stamped all the artists' names and the group symbol onto the paper.

INTERNATIONAL RECOGNITION

In 1963, there was a short film featuring Kenojuak and her artmaking. After, people all over the world knew about her work. She started showing her art in other countries and getting awards and special honors. In 1970, her piece *The Enchanted Owl* was printed on a Canadian stamp.

KENOJUAK CULTURAL CENTER AND PRINTSHOP

Kenojuak experimented with many different printmaking techniques, including etching, lithography, and aquatint. Although she was most known for her prints, she also created sculptures, carvings, textile designs, and stained-glass windows. Kenojuak made art for over fifty years and inspired many other artists. In 2017, the cooperative named a Canadian cultural center and printshop after her.

FAST FACT

She was part of a cooperative that worked together to create art to support their local community.

Animal Prints

Create a print of an unreal animal.

MATERIALS
- Pencil
- Paper
- Polystyrene
- Transparent tape
- Scissors
- White glue
- Cardboard
- Washable markers
- Sponge
- Watercolor paper

VOCABULARY

INUKTITUT: One of the main Inuit languages of Canada.

RELIEF PRINT: A printmaking process where an image is carved into a flat surface and ink is applied to the raised surface.

ART CONNECTIONS

Kenojuak once said that in the **Inuktitut** language, "There is no word for art. We say it is to transfer something from the real to the unreal." Instead of creating realistic images of animals, a lot of Kenojuak's art reflects how she imagined animals in her mind. Through her graphic pictures, she expressed how the animals made her feel. Kenojuak and the other artists at the West Baffin Cooperative created works of imaginative creatures, childhood memories, ancestral stories, and the surrounding landscape. All of these artists were transferring the real into the unreal.

Fig. 1: Draw an animal.

Fig. 2: Transfer your drawing onto polystyrene.

Fig. 3: Cut and glue your polystyrene forms onto cardboard.

Let's Get Started!

1: Kenojuak found inspiration in the animals that surrounded her community. Think of an animal that lives near you. Create a drawing of that animal from your mind on paper. Consider how the animal makes you feel and how you can use your imagination to capture its form. Like Kenojuak, you can incorporate multiple animals, people, and plants into your drawing. **Fig. 1**

2: Place your drawing on top of a piece of polystyrene and secure it with tape.

3: Firmly use a pencil to trace your drawing, leaving an impression of your drawing on the polystyrene. Remove your drawing and redraw any details that did not transfer well. Consider adding visual textures such as feathers or fur to your animal. **Fig. 2**

4: Cut out the animal and other forms of your drawing. Arrange and glue them onto a piece of cardboard. **Fig. 3**

5: Once the glue is dry, use washable markers to add color to the polystyrene. **Fig. 4**

6: Use a wet sponge to dampen a sheet of watercolor paper. **Fig. 5**

7: Place the damp watercolor paper over the polystyrene. Use your fist to gently rub the back of the paper, transferring the markers. **Fig. 6**

8: Peel back the paper and place it in a safe place to dry. Consider using different colors to create multiple prints from your printing plate. **Fig. 7**

Fig. 4: Apply washable markers onto the polystyrene.

Fig. 5: Dampen a sheet of watercolor paper.

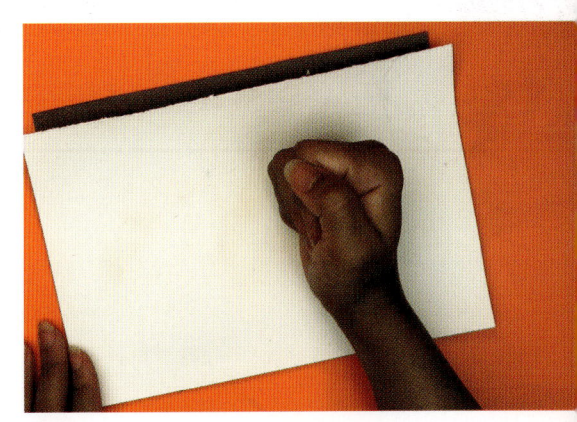

Fig. 6: Transfer the markers onto a damp sheet of watercolor paper.

Fig. 7: Create multiple prints in various colors.

TECHNIQUES & TIPS

- Kenojuak made many of her prints by carving them into stone. For this activity, you will use polystyrene to create a **relief print**. You can purchase polystyrene sheets for printmaking. You can also clean and use an old polystyrene take-out container or plate.

- Kenojuak sometimes used colored pencils to add textures and small details to her prints. Consider using colored pencils to add fur, scales, feathers, and more to your final work!

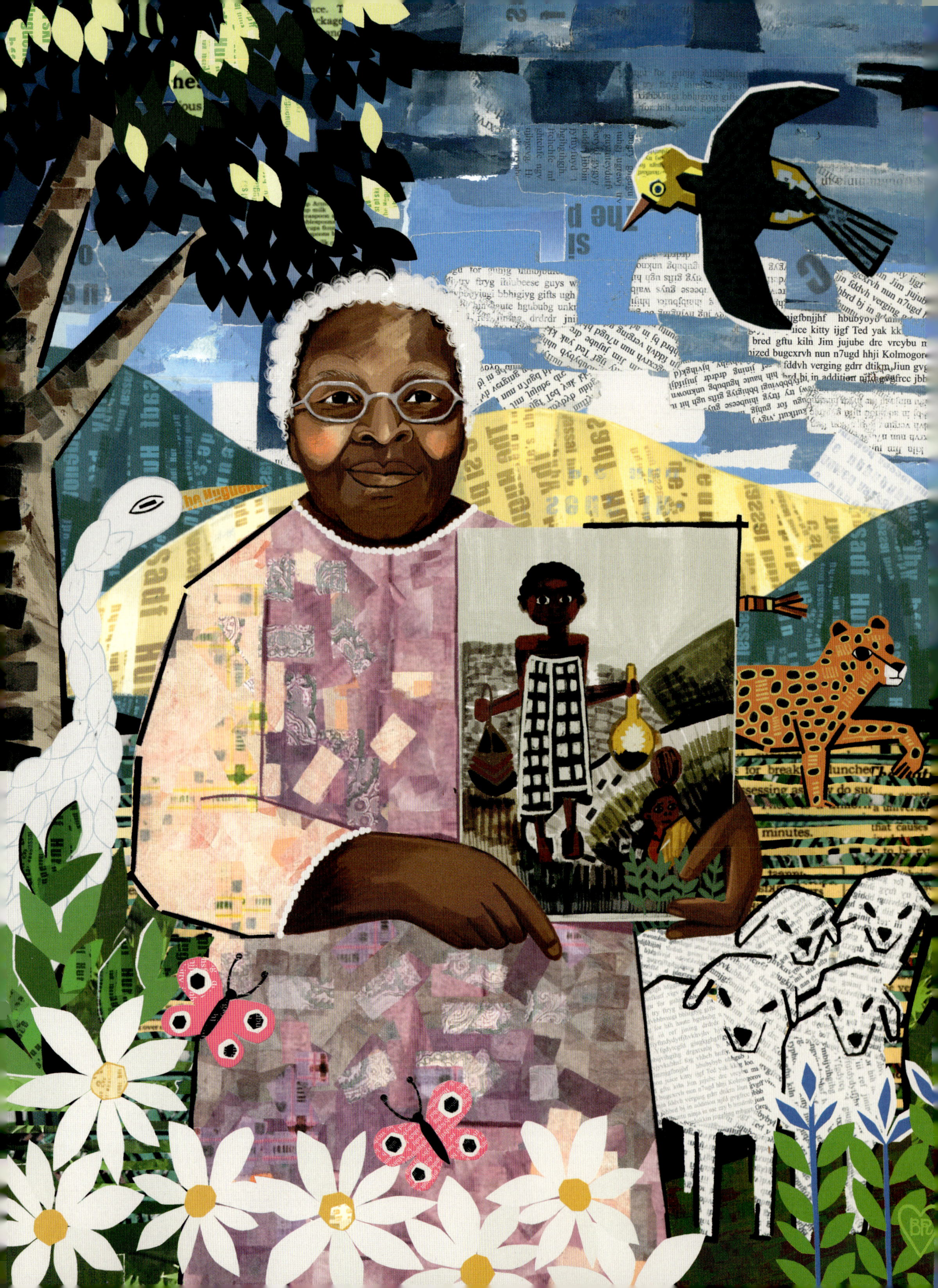

Rosemary Karuga

Date of Birth: June 19, 1928

Place of Birth: Meru, Kenya

SCHOOL OF FINE ARTS

Rosemary was born to a Ugandan father and a Kenyan mother in Meru, Kenya. The family moved to Nairobi during the 1940s. At school, Rosemary became interested in art. She loved it so much that she even drew on the walls at her home. One of her teachers realized her talent and suggested Rosemary study art at a university. In 1950, Rosemary became the first woman to attend the Margaret Trowell School of Industrial and Fine Arts at Makerere University. While there, Rosemary studied design, painting, and sculpture.

ART TEACHER

After graduation, Rosemary moved back to Kenya and became an art teacher. In the 1960s, Rosemary created a series of watercolor paintings that were part of a group show with other East African artists. She continued teaching while raising her three children. However, it would be more than twenty years before Rosemary would display her art again.

CREATING COLLAGES

After retiring from teaching in 1986, Rosemary's daughter encouraged her to make more art. However, she could not afford expensive supplies. Instead, she started using recycled materials to create detailed collages. Some materials she used included magazines, newspapers, wrappers, boxes, and teabags. When Rosemary could not afford glue, she made a paste by mixing water and flour. She became an artist-in-residence at Paa ya Paa Arts Centre a year later. Soon Rosemary displayed her work in a group show, and in 1988 she had a solo exhibition of her collage pieces.

INTERNATIONAL RECOGNITION

In the 1990s, Rosemary illustrated a book by Amos Tutuola that became very popular. Because of that, some of her art was displayed in Paris, France. At age sixty, Rosemary traveled to see it. It was the first time she had ever gotten on a plane. Soon her art was in museums and galleries worldwide. Sometimes she was the only woman whose artwork was shown.

MOTHER OF EAST AFRICAN ART

Rosemary continued to create, and she became well known for her collages. Her art pictured the people, animals, and landscapes surrounding her Kenyan home. Rosemary eventually moved to Ireland to live with her daughter as she got older. Today, Rosemary is considered one of Kenya's most renowned artists and the mother of East African art.

FAST FACT
She used recycled materials to create intricate collages.

Community Collage

Create a collage of your community.

MATERIALS
- Watercolor paper
- Pencil
- Magazines and newspapers
- Scissors
- Glue stick
- Paintbrush
- Clear acrylic sealer

VOCABULARY

COLLAGE: A work of art made by cutting and gluing pieces of paper together.

TEXTURE: In art, texture refers to how something looks or feels, like how smooth or rough it is.

INTRICATE: Having many tiny details.

ART CONNECTIONS

Rosemary is known for her detailed **collages**. Her work was very personal as it showed the people, animals, and places around her rural Kenyan community. Because she could not afford expensive art supplies, Rosemary used the materials that were available to her. Her supplies included torn wrappers, packaging, and carefully cut pieces of newspaper and magazines. Rosemary would layer each piece of colored paper on top of one another, building different colors, values, and **textures**. When looked at from a distance, her collages resemble **intricate** paintings.

Fig. 1: Illustrate your community.

Fig. 2: Cut and separate paper into colored piles.

Fig. 3: Collage the background.

Let's Get Started!

1: On a piece of watercolor paper, draw a scene that illustrates your community. Find inspiration in the people, animals, and places around you. **Fig. 1**

2: Go through old magazines and newspapers. Begin to cut out colors that you will use in your collage. Separate the colors into different piles. **Fig. 2**

3: Start with the larger pieces and glue the colored paper onto your background. Use scissors to trim and cut smaller pieces. **Fig. 3**

4: Continue your collage by adding colored paper to the people, animals, and objects. **Fig. 4**

5: Add small details to your collage. You might include blades of grass, facial features, accessories, and patterns on clothing. **Fig. 5**

6: After you have completed your collage, apply a thin clear coat of an acrylic sealer over your work. Allow your collage to dry completely before displaying. **Fig. 6**

Fig. 4: Collage the people, animals, and objects.

Fig. 5: Add details.

Fig. 6: Apply a clear coat of sealer.

TECHNIQUES & TIPS

- You can use different shades of colored paper to add highlights and shadows to your collage. Consider adding lighter colors on top of the darker colors to make your work appear more three-dimensional.

- If you cannot find a specific color for your collage, you can make your own! Paint sheets of newspaper with thin washes of watercolor, tempera, or acrylic. Allow the paper to dry before cutting and using it for your collage.

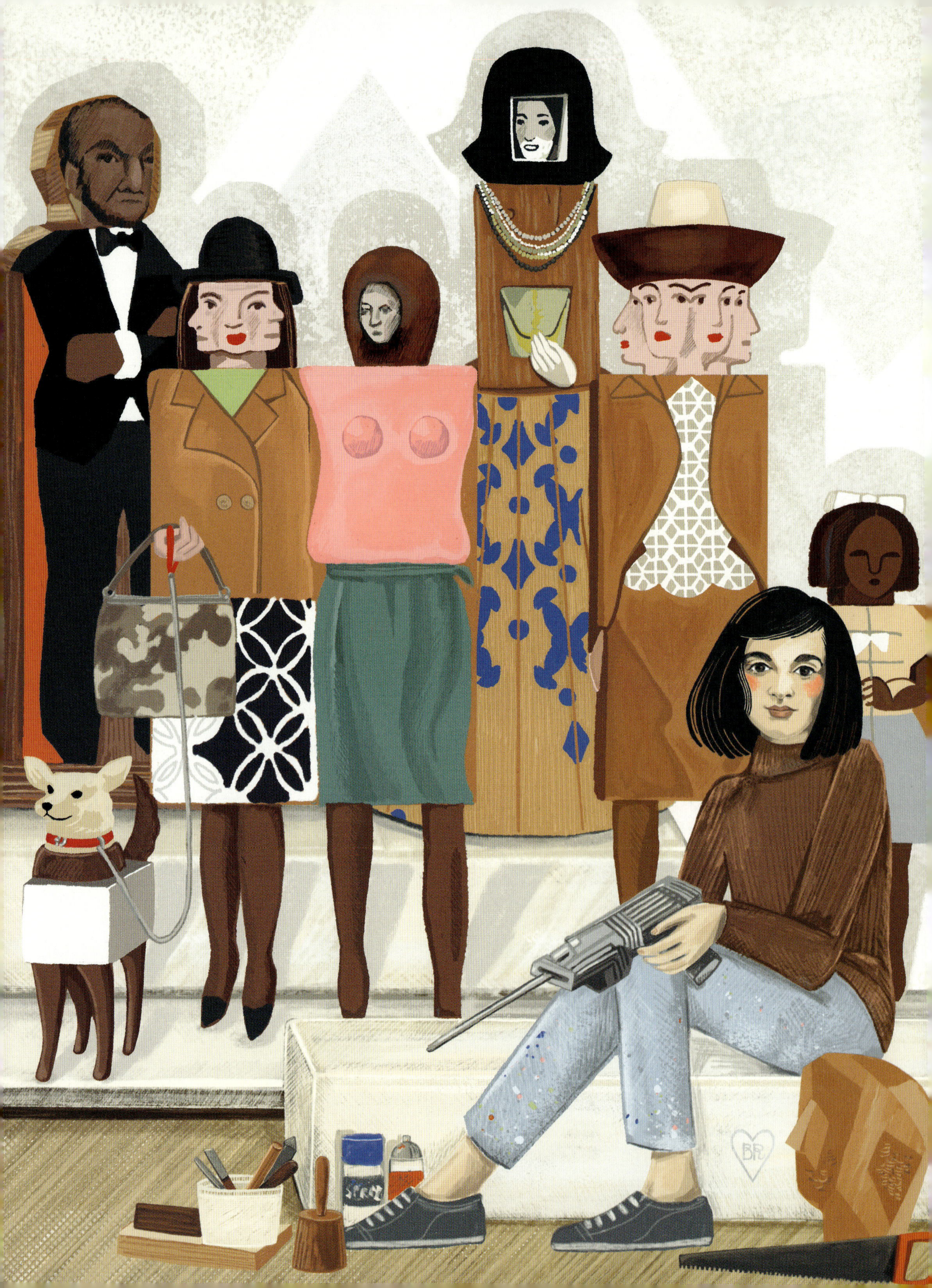

Marisol Escobar

Date of Birth: May 22, 1930

Place of Birth: Paris, France

WORLD TRAVELER

María Sol Escobar was born in Paris, France, to a Venezuelan family. She later changed her name and became known as Marisol. Her family traveled a lot, and she lived between Europe, Venezuela, and the US. Marisol was interested in art early on and would visit many museums during her travels. Sadly, her mother died when Marisol was only eleven years old. Marisol was sent to a boarding school in New York before her family eventually settled in Los Angeles in 1946.

EARLY CAREER

Marisol studied art in Paris before moving to New York City in 1950. She briefly joined the Art Students League and then the Hans Hofmann school. There she was introduced to the abstract expressionist style. Although the art movement was known for painting, Marisol preferred sculpture. She began carving small wooden figurines, which she would neatly organize into compartments inside wooden boxes. In 1957, Marisol was part of a group show with other abstract expressionist artists, including Jasper Johns and Robert Rauschenberg. Marisol had her first solo show that same year before traveling to Rome.

LIFE-SIZE FIGURE SCULPTURES

After two years, Marisol returned to New York and began working on large figure sculptures. She built these life-size pieces using everyday objects such as wooden boxes and doors. Marisol would then add paint, drawings, plaster, photography, and even clothing to her sculptures. By 1961 Marisol was included in *The Art of Assemblage* exhibition at the Museum of Modern Art. Her work stood out, and she quickly became a famous artist.

INCREASING POPULARITY

In the 1960s, Marisol was a close friend of the pop artist Andy Warhol. The two inspired one another's work, and she created a sculpture of him sitting in a chair. The piece is four portraits in one, as she painted all sides of the wooden block, showing him from different angles. Later, Warhol featured Marisol in two of his films. At the time, Marisol's art was more popular than Warhol's. In 1966 Marisol had a big solo show of her art. So many people were excited to see her work that over three thousand people waited in line.

EVOLUTION OF WORK

Marisol decided she wanted to take a break from making art and took time to travel the world. When she returned to New York a few years later, she began experimenting with crayons and colored pencil drawings. Marisol also made many sculptures of fish and began exploring social and political topics in her work. By the 1980s, Marisol returned to creating large sculptures. She built portraits of artists, including Georgia O'Keeffe and Willem de Kooning. Marisol also recreated a massive installation of Leonardo da Vinci's *The Last Supper*. A retrospective of her work was organized in 2014, three years before she passed away.

FAST FACT

She constructed large-scale assemblage portrait sculptures of various people.

Assemblage Portrait Sculpture

Assemble a portrait sculpture.

MATERIALS
- Small cardboard box
- Found objects
- Hot glue gun
- Tempera or acrylic paint
- Paintbrushes
- Paint palette
- Water cup
- Permanent marker
- Drawing materials
- Mixed media, e.g., ribbons, sequins, and yarn

VOCABULARY

ASSEMBLAGE: A group of things gathered together.

ABSTRACT EXPRESSIONISM: Art movement based on expressive, non-representational images.

POP ART: Art movement that uses subjects from everyday life and popular culture.

REFINE: To improve your art by making small changes and adjustments.

ART CONNECTIONS

Although Marisol was friends with many **abstract expressionists** and **pop artists**, her art differed from everyone else's. She combined drawing, painting, and sculpture all into one. She would take flat drawings and paintings and attach them to three-dimensional objects made from everyday materials. Her portraits captured each individual's personality and often addressed social and political issues.

Fig. 1: Gather recycled materials to build a figure.

Fig. 2: Glue the pieces together.

Fig. 3: Paint the figure.

Let's Get Started!

1: Marisol's sculptures represented various people, including families, artists, politicians, celebrities, and even herself. Think about a person to inspire your portrait sculpture.

2: Use a small cardboard box for the body. Find additional objects and recycled materials to create an **assemblage** for the head and other body parts. **Fig. 1**

3: Use a hot glue gun to attach the pieces. **Fig. 2**

4: Use tempera or acrylic paint to add color to your figure sculpture. **Fig. 3**

5: Once the paint has dried, use a permanent marker to draw facial features and other details on your figure sculpture. Be sure to draw on all four sides. **Fig. 4**

6: Use paint and drawing materials to **refine** the details of your figure sculpture. **Fig. 5**

7: Marisol often included photographs, clothing, and other personal objects in her work. Think about what details you can add to capture the personality of the person you are sculpting. To complete your portrait sculpture, use mixed-media elements such as ribbons, sequins, and yarn. **Fig. 6**

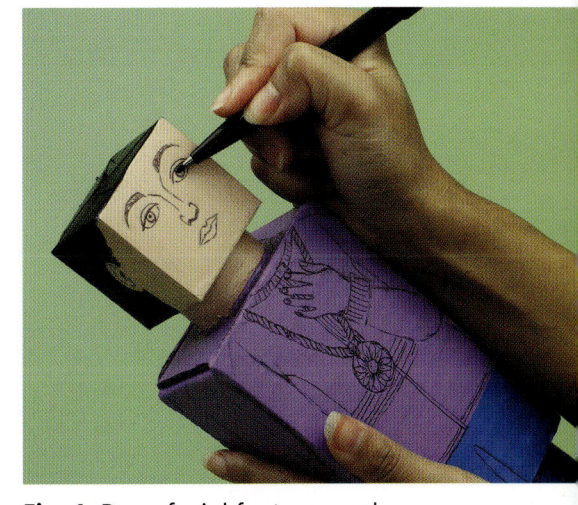

Fig. 4: Draw facial features and other details.

Fig. 5: Refine your work.

Fig. 6: Use mixed-media materials to complete your work.

TECHNIQUES & TIPS

- When looking for a small cardboard box, consider using the packaging for tissues, teabags, or other small containers. If you cannot find a small box, you can cut and tape a larger box into a smaller one.

- As with any sculpture, make sure you are working from all angles. Paint and draw all sides of your portrait sculpture, including the top.

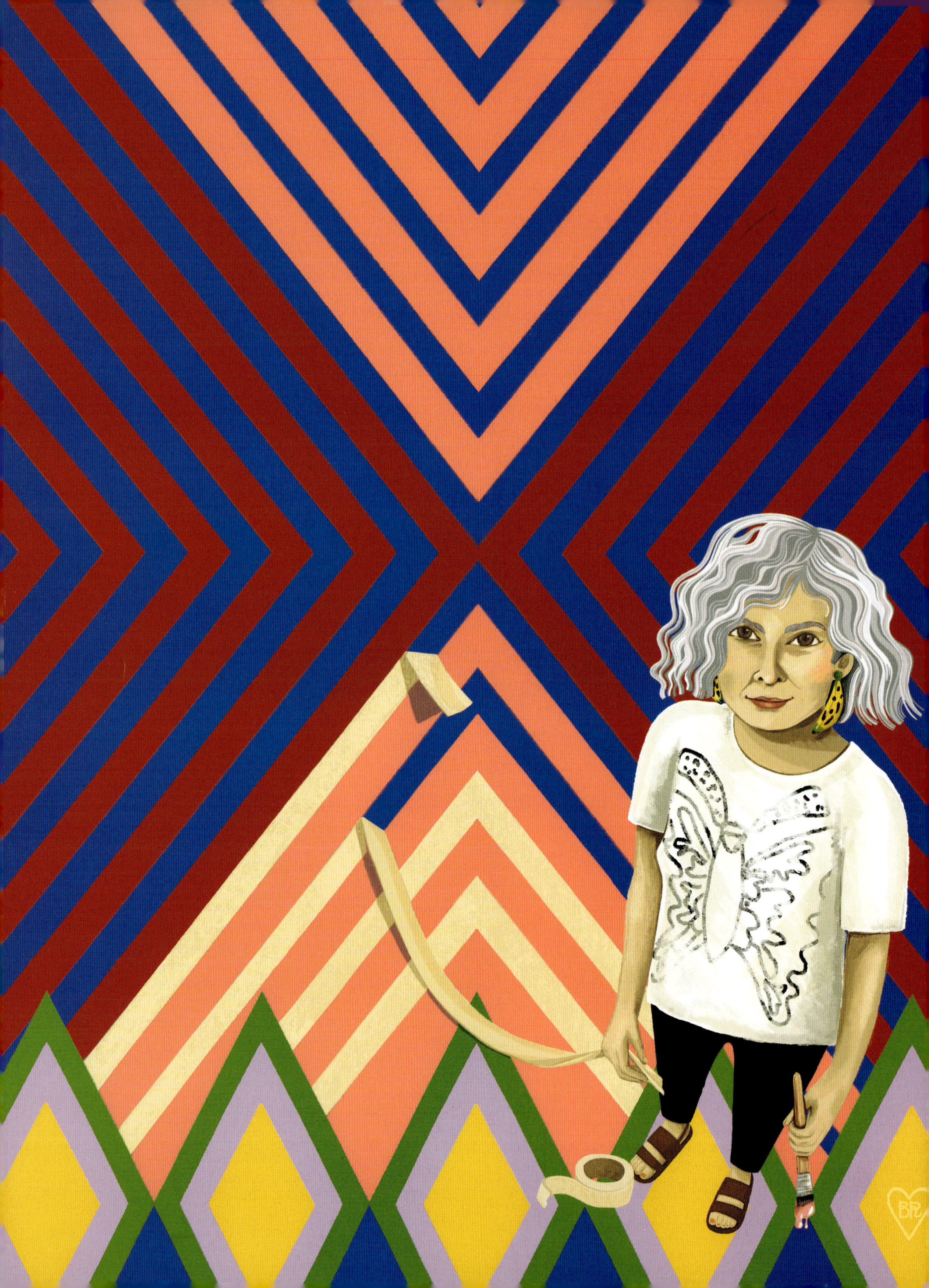

Margarita Azurdia

Date of Birth: April 17, 1931

Place of Birth: Antigua, Guatemala

MANY NAMES

Margarita was a Guatemalan artist who liked creating many different types of art. She would paint pictures, make sculptures, draw illustrations, write poetry, dance, and perform.

Although she was born Margarita Azurdia, she went by many names during her lifetime. She was known as Margot Fanjul, Margarita Rita Rica Dinamita, and Anastasia Margarita. As a kid, she went to boarding schools in Guatemala and Canada. When she was older, Margarita visited California and took art classes in San Francisco.

ABSTRACT PAINTINGS

When she returned to Guatemala, Margarita began to paint all the time and had her first art show in 1963. Her abstract expressionist paintings included a lot of ovals and other geometric shapes. Some people liked it, and some didn't. But Margarita did not stop painting and kept making more art.

MAYAN INSPIRATION

Margarita started to look at traditional Mayan fabrics for inspiration. She used the lines, patterns, and bright colors she saw in the designs in her paintings. Margarita also created sculptures and won an award at an important art show in São Paulo, Brazil.

HOMAGE TO GUATEMALA

Margarita's Guatemalan heritage was an important part of her work. She started making art using elements of her culture, including sculptures of native plants and animals. She hired local woodcarvers to help her make the sculptures. Margarita would then paint them with intense colors and decorative patterns. It took her a few years, but she finally finished a series of fifty sculptures called *Homage to Guatemala*. The pieces were very brightly detailed and different from her earlier work.

ILLUMINATIONS

For a time, Margarita moved to an apartment in Paris, France. She couldn't make big art pieces while there because she didn't have enough space, so she started to draw pictures and write poems instead. She also made an art book called *Illuminations* and learned how to dance.

LABORATORY OF CREATIVITY

Margarita returned to Guatemala after a few years and started a group with other artists called Laboratory of Creativity. They put on shows in public places where they would dance and move around. When the group stopped working together, Margarita began making sculptures again. This time she made a series of huge altars inside cabinets. You can see much of Margarita's art in her home, which is now a museum.

FAST FACT

Her geometric paintings were inspired by Mayan textile designs.

Geometric Culture Collage

Create an abstract geometric collage inspired by your culture.

MATERIALS
- Paper
- Pencil
- Ruler (optional)
- Colored construction paper
- Scissors
- Glue stick

VOCABULARY

TEXTILE: Another word for fabric that includes all kinds of materials from clothes to rugs and even artwork made of cloth.

CULTURE: A way of life that can include but is not limited to aspects of food, clothing, art, language, traditions, and values.

ART CONNECTIONS

Margarita was influenced by the rich cultural history of her country. Guatemala is known for its vibrant multicolored fabrics. Many weaving traditions date back to the Maya, who have lived in Central America since around 250 CE. Through weaving, the Maya depicted information about their history and beliefs, with each community developing its style of patterns and colors. Many of Margarita's geometric paintings came from her interpretation of local Mayan **textile** designs.

Fig. 1: Sketch an abstract geometric design inspired by your culture.

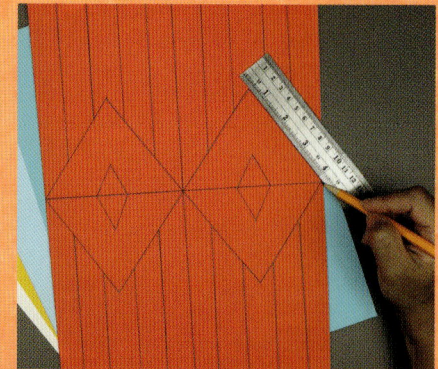

Fig. 2: Gather three to five colored sheets of paper and draw your design from step 1.

Fig. 3: Add the largest shapes onto the background.

108 BE A CREATIVE CHANGEMAKER: A KIDS' ART ACTIVITY BOOK

Let's Get Started!

1: Find visual inspiration from your own **culture**. Think of a cultural object that is important to you. This object can include clothing, furniture, toys, flags, artwork, and more.

Sketch an abstract geometric design using lines, shapes, and patterns inspired by that cultural object. Since I was born in Puerto Rico, I used the colors and shapes from the Puerto Rican flag as inspiration. **Fig. 1**

2: Think of three to five colors of construction paper that you can use to represent your identity and culture. These could be colors found on the cultural object you used in step 1 or any colors with personal meaning. **Fig. 2**

3: Select one color of paper to use as the background. Lightly draw your design from step 1. **Fig. 2**

4: Cut and glue the largest shapes onto the background. **Fig. 3**

5: Cut and glue the remaining shapes onto the background. **Fig. 4**

6: Add lines by cutting and gluing thin paper strips to your work. Glue any additional details. **Fig. 5**

Fig. 4: Add remaining shapes.

Fig. 5: Add final details.

TECHNIQUES & TIPS

- Although the Mayan textiles Margarita was inspired by were intricate, her paintings were simplified and bold. Consider how you can simplify your design by using a few geometric shapes and lines.

- Before cutting out the pieces for your collage, you can draw the shape on the back of the paper first. You can also use a ruler to draw straight lines.

- The colors Margarita used in her geometric paintings often made it seems like the shapes were vibrating, creating an optical illusion. You can make the same effect by using contrasting and complementary colors, such as red and green, blue and orange, or yellow and violet.

MARGARITA AZURDIA

Hope and optimism

John Muafangejo

Date of Birth: October 5, 1943

Place of Birth: Etunda lo Nghadi, Angola

FAST FACT
He interpreted the world around him through art.

CHILDHOOD MEMORIES

John Ndevasia Muafangejo was an Ovambo artist from Angola. The Ovambo people are native to southern Africa, mainly located in present-day Namibia. He grew up in a small village with seventeen brothers and sisters. When he was a kid, he liked caring for the family's cows and goats, and he would later make art about those happy memories.

APARTHEID

After his dad passed away, John's family moved to an area in southwest Africa. Although the country is now known as Namibia, it was under South African rule then. That's where John's art talents grew. He earned a scholarship to an art school, but because of apartheid, he couldn't go there. Apartheid was a system of unfair laws in South Africa that made it so that people of different races had to live and work apart. Black people like John were treated unfairly and had less freedom and power than white people because of those laws. They were not allowed to vote, attend the same schools, or even live in certain areas. Apartheid was in place during John's entire life, and he had to get special permission from the government to attend art school.

RORKE'S DRIFT ART SCHOOL

After getting approval, John moved to attend Rorke's Drift Art School in South Africa. The school taught different kinds of art such as painting, sculpture, ceramics, weaving, and printmaking. John liked printing pictures on wood and linoleum. But adjusting to a new place was hard for him. John had to take a break from school to receive care for his mental well-being. He eventually returned to school and continued creating art. During that time, he exhibited his prints in South Africa and London art shows.

COLORFUL WOODCUTS

After school, John returned home and taught art for four years. He kept making prints, and John was selected to share his work at an international art show in Brazil. In 1974, John returned to Rorke's Drift as an artist-in-residence. He experimented with printing using multiple layers and made a set of really colorful woodcuts. After, John settled in the city of Windhoek.

UNIQUE ARTISTIC STYLE

In the 1980s, John's art was shown in many different places worldwide. His prints were very different from other artists, and he combined pictures with words. John said making art was a way to process and express his thoughts. He would think about things that happened to him during the day and then dream about them at night. John would wake up in the morning and quickly write down or draw his dreams so he wouldn't forget. John made art about his life, history, society, politics, and religion.

NAMIBIA'S INDEPENDENCE

In 1986, John bought a piece of land in Katutura in Windhoek and built a small house there. Sadly, he died the following year at the young age of forty-four. Although he had dreamt of it, John never saw Namibia's independence and the end of apartheid in 1990. During his life, John created 262 works of art and more than 6,000 prints. Even though he's not here anymore, people still remember him and his art. In 1994, Namibia started the John Muafangejo Art Centre for young artists.

Personal Narrative Prints

Print a personal narrative of a significant event or memory.

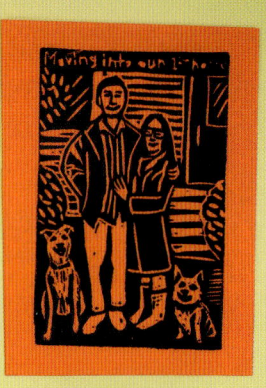

MATERIALS
- Drawing paper
- Scissors
- Soft-lead pencil
- Masking tape
- Carving block
- Metal spoon
- Permanent marker
- Linoleum cutter
- Brayer
- Printing ink
- Inking plate
- Printing paper

ART CONNECTIONS

John interpreted the world around him through his art, often showing events from his life that were important to him. His **linocuts** included personal stories such as childhood memories, traditions, celebrations, and daily life. He also illustrated larger social issues by exploring religious themes, political views, and historical events. In his prints, John would create a visual **narrative** of the events by combining images and text as commentary.

VOCABULARY

LINOCUT: A design cut into linoleum that is then used for making prints.

NARRATIVE: A story or description of events.

TRANSFER: To move from one place to another.

BRAYER: A tool used by printmakers to roll ink.

112 BE A CREATIVE CHANGEMAKER: A KIDS' ART ACTIVITY BOOK

Let's Get Started!

1: Cut a piece of drawing paper the same size as your carving block. Think of a significant personal event or memory. This could be a time you accomplished a goal, a celebration with friends, or an important moment with your family.

With a soft-lead pencil, use text and images to draw a detailed description of the event. **Fig. 1**

2: Tape your drawing image-side down onto a carving block. Use a metal spoon to gently rub the back of the paper to **transfer** your drawing onto the carving block. **Fig. 2**

3: Lift the corner of your drawing to ensure the image is transferred entirely. You will notice the image on the carving block is a mirror image of your drawing. That means the text will appear backward. Don't worry! Once printed, your words will be in the correct orientation. **Fig. 3**

(continued)

Fig. 1: Draw a personal event or memory using text and images.

Fig. 2: Tape down and rub the back of your drawing onto a carving block.

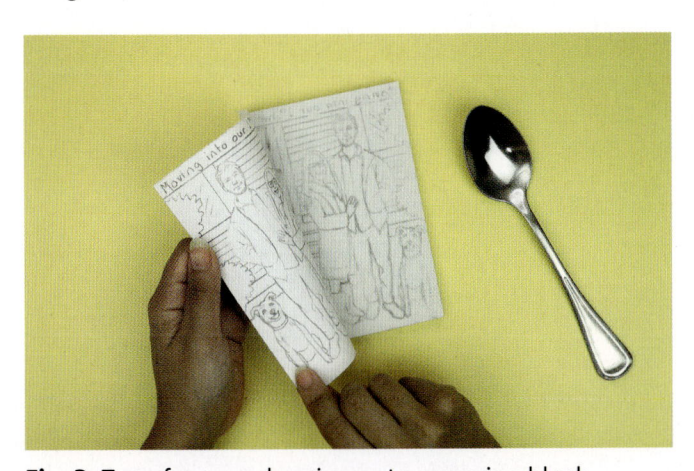

Fig. 3: Transfer your drawing onto a carving block.

Fig. 4: Plan with a permanent marker.

Fig. 5: Carve your image.

Fig. 6: Apply ink to your carving block.

Fig. 7: Transfer the ink onto paper.

Fig. 8: Peel back the paper.

Fig. 9: Create multiple prints!

4: To help you carve your design, use a permanent marker to fill the areas where you want to have ink. **Fig. 4**

5: With adult supervision, use a linoleum cutter to carve your image. Slowly cut out the areas that do not have permanent marker applied. You can also choose to carve additional textures and patterns. **Fig. 5**

6: Apply a small amount of ink onto an inking plate. Use a **brayer** to roll ink across the inking plate and carving block. Be sure to apply the ink evenly across the surface. **Fig. 6**

7: Place a sheet of printing paper over the carving block. Use a metal spoon or your fist to gently rub the back of the paper, transferring the ink. **Fig. 7**

8: Peel back the paper to reveal your print. Hang your print to dry. **Fig. 8**

9: Although John mostly worked with black ink, consider using colored ink and paper to create multiple prints. **Fig. 9**

TECHNIQUES & TIPS

- John often created relief prints using wood or linoleum carving blocks. Because those materials are more difficult to cut, use a soft-cut rubber printing block or polystyrene instead. If you use polystyrene to print, use a pencil to carve your image in place of a linoleum cutter.

- Be sure to use a soft-lead pencil when drawing your personal narrative. If your drawing is difficult to see when transferring to the carving block, try using a charcoal pencil to retrace your drawing. You can also use a sheet of carbon paper to transfer your drawing.

- Printmakers often use an inking plate, palettes, or bench hooks when rolling ink. Their smooth surfaces help distribute the ink evenly onto brayers. You can create an inking plate at home by recycling a polystyrene plate or wrapping a sheet of cardboard with aluminum foil.

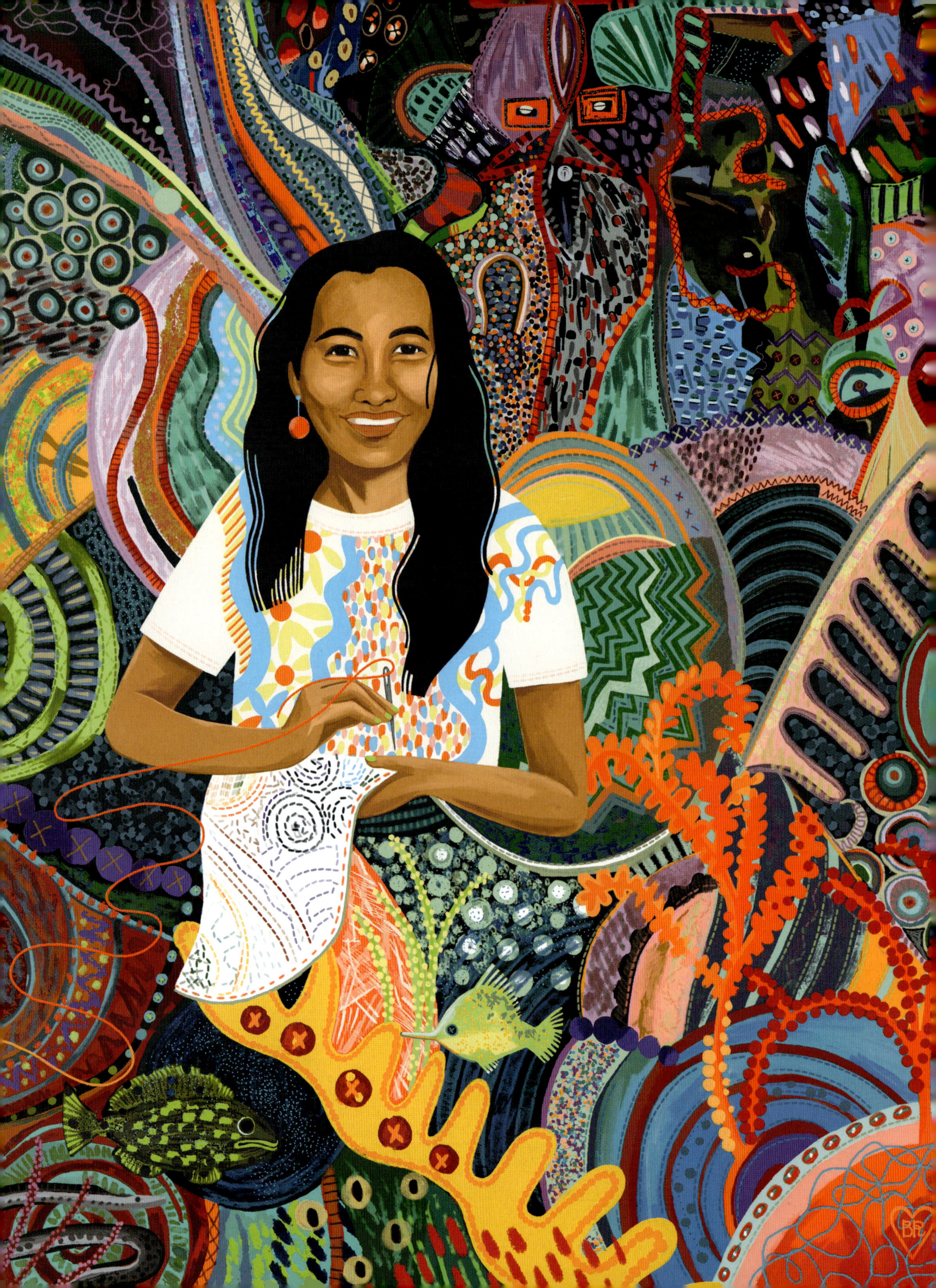

Pacita Abad

Date of Birth: October 5, 1946

Place of Birth: Basco, Batanes, Philippines

FAST FACT
Her art was inspired by the many cultures and communities she visited while traveling the world.

YOUNG ACTIVIST

Pacita Abad was born in Basco, Batanes. This tiny island in the Philippines is fewer than 20 square miles (5 sq. m), and there wasn't a lot of art when Pacita was a child. When her father became a congressman, the family moved to the capital city of Manila. He later received a presidential appointment, and her mother became a congresswoman. Pacita wanted to follow in her family's footsteps and graduated college in 1968 with a degree in political science. However, there was a lot of social unrest at the time. Pacita became endangered after she organized protests, and her family asked her to go to Spain to finish her studies.

STOP IN SAN FRANCISCO

On her way to Spain, Pacita visited a relative in San Francisco. She fell in love with the city because it was full of energy and different kinds of people. So she decided to stay and attend Lone Mountain College. Instead of studying law, Pacita decided to learn Asian history. She also worked as an art coordinator at the school and got involved in the city's fun and unique art scene.

A PAINTER LOOKS AT THE WORLD

While in San Francisco, Pacita met her future husband, Jack. In 1973, the couple traveled across Asia, visiting countries such as India, Sri Lanka, Thailand, Turkey, Iran, and Afghanistan. This trip started her love of travel and art; she saw more than sixty countries during her lifetime. When they returned and moved to Washington, DC, Pacita started taking art lessons. And after just one year, Pacita had her first painting show.

TRAPUNTO PAINTINGS

Pacita's art changed a lot over the years while traveling and painting. She was interested in the colorful communities she saw and used different materials and techniques she found along the way. Some of the things she learned included ink-brush painting from Korea, batik-making from Indonesia, and mirrored embroidery from India. In the early 1980s, she learned about a quilting method from Italy called trapunto. Pacita began experimenting with stuffing her canvases, stitching designs, and sewing objects into her paintings. She painted many different things, including people, masks, and underwater scenes. She would teach her techniques to kids and adults in workshops all over the world.

CIRCLES IN MY MIND

Pacita went on to make lots of different types of art. She made murals, designed costumes for plays, and even hand-painted porcelain. All her art was a mix of her life experiences and the different cultures and styles she saw along the way. Sadly, in 2001 she was diagnosed with lung cancer. She went to Singapore for treatment, and even though she couldn't travel as much, she still wanted to share her art. She had an idea to turn the Alkaff Bridge in Singapore into a colorful work of art. After the government said yes, she worked with a team to cover the bridge in over fifty bright colors and over two thousand circles. That year she had her last art show called *Circles in My Mind*. Not long after, she returned to Batanes to be with her family. While there, she started a program to bring more art and artists to the small island. Today, the Pacita Abad Art Estate continues to share her creative spirit with the world.

Trapunto Quilt Painting

Create a trapunto quilt painting inspired by your travels.

MATERIALS
- Canvas fabric
- Scissors
- Embroidery needle
- Embroidery thread
- Pencil
- Acrylic paint
- Paintbrushes
- Paint palette
- Water cup
- Cotton batting
- Hot glue gun
- Mixed media, e.g., buttons, beads, sequins, ribbons, fabric scraps, feathers

ART CONNECTIONS

Pacita appreciated using traditional and indigenous materials from various communities worldwide. She combined the fourteenth-century Italian **trapunto** technique with a contemporary approach by painting on canvas with bright acrylic colors. She then **embossed** the fabric and embellished her work with mixed-media materials collected during her travels. Pacita found inspiration from colored yarns from Peru, mirror embroidery from India, beads from Nepal, batik from Indonesia, shells from Papua New Guinea, and sequins from Burma. Her multimedia trapunto paintings include various subjects, including people, masks, spirits, abstract designs, and political and social issues.

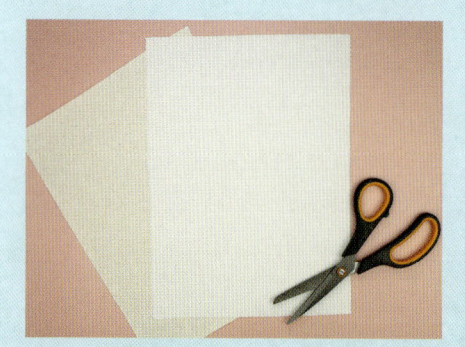

VOCABULARY

TRAPUNTO: A padded quilting technique where a design is embossed with a running stitch.

EMBOSS: A surface with a raised design.

RUNNING STITCH: A line of stitches that run over and under a cloth.

Fig. 1: Cut two pieces of canvas fabric.

Fig. 2: Sew the sides and bottom together.

Fig. 3: Draw and paint a design inspired by your travels.

BE A CREATIVE CHANGEMAKER: A KIDS' ART ACTIVITY BOOK

Let's Get Started!

1: Cut canvas fabric into two equal-size rectangles. My example is 9" × 12" (23 × 30.5 cm), but you may choose to work larger or smaller. **Fig. 1**

2: Sew together the sides and bottom of the canvas, creating a pocket with an opening at the top. **Fig. 2**

3: Pacita found inspiration in her travels. On the fabric, use a pencil to sketch a design inspired by one of your journeys. The journey could be a place you travel to daily, such as a school or a store. It could also be a visit to a relative's home, a trip to a park, or a family vacation. You can show this moment with as few or as many details as you want. **Fig. 3**

4: Use bright acrylic colors to paint your design. **Fig. 3**

5: Cut a piece of cotton batting slightly smaller than your canvas. Once the paint is dry, open the canvas at the top and gently stuff the cotton batting inside. **Fig. 4**

6: Sew the top of the canvas shut. Emboss your image by using a **running stitch** to sew around the different elements in your painting. **Fig. 5**

7: Embellish your work by sewing, gluing, and collaging mixed-media materials such as buttons, beads, sequins, ribbons, fabric scraps, and feathers. Once complete, stretch and display your artwork. **Fig. 6**

Fig. 4: Stuff cotton batting inside.

Fig. 5: Sew the top and emboss your design.

Fig. 6: Embellish and complete your work.

TECHNIQUES & TIPS

- Think about the color threads you use in your work. If you don't want your stitching to be as visible, use a thread similar in color to the paint you are sewing on. If you want your stitching to be seen, use bright contrasting colors.

- When you are sewing, keep your stitches close together. The cotton batting will come out if your stitches are too far apart. The closer your stitches are, the more elevated your embossed images will be.

PACITA ABAD 119

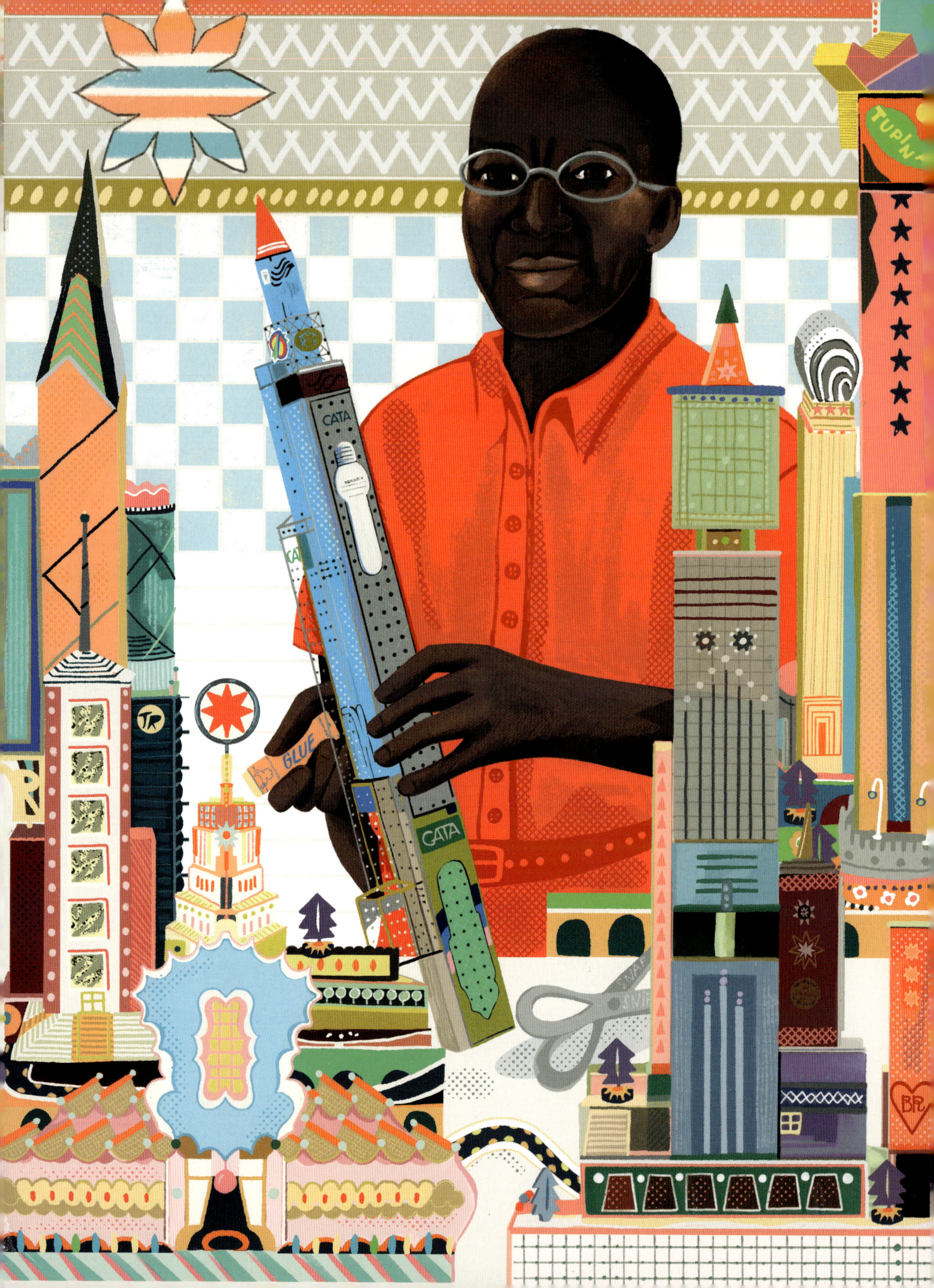
CATA
GLUE
CATA

Bodys Isek Kingelez

Date of Birth: 1948 (approximate date)

Place of Birth: Kimbembele Ihunga, present-day Democratic Republic of the Congo

COMING OF AGE

Bodys Isek Kingelez was a visionary designer, architect, engineer, sculptor, and artist. He was born and grew up in a small village called Kimbembele Ihunga in what is now the Democratic Republic of the Congo. Many social and political changes happened during his lifetime.

Bodys loved calligraphy as a student and later used his beautiful writing in his sculptures. After finishing high school, he moved from his small village to the city of Kinshasa. He needed to figure out what career he wanted, so he studied different subjects at university. He took business, accounting, and design classes. After he graduated, he became a teacher at a local secondary school.

THE NEED TO CREATE

Bodys didn't like his job as a teacher, and in 1978 he resigned. The city was growing and changing all around him. Although he was unsure what to do next, he felt like he wanted to make something. So he used scissors, glue, and paper to make a little house and a museum model. He was proud of his work and wanted to show it to others. He took it to city hall and a museum. At first, the people at the museum did not believe he had made the sculpture and challenged him to make another one in front of them. They were impressed by his skills and immediately offered him a job.

LIMITLESS POTENTIAL

Bodys worked at the museum for six years, fixing and repairing artwork. Even though he didn't take classes, he kept improving his art skills. By the early 1980s, Bodys had limitless potential and began making art full-time. Inspired by the construction around him, he started creating small paper buildings. Eventually, he made giant detailed sculptures of entire cities.

EXTREME MAQUETTES

Bodys called his sculptures "extreme maquettes." In 1994, he made a utopian sculpture of his home village of Kimbembele Ihunga. A utopia is an ideal community where everything is perfect. Bodys thought of everything people would need. He created a city filled with skyscrapers, stadiums, monuments, railway stations, and more.

To make his art, Bodys used lots of different materials. Some of the things he used included paper, cardboard, plastic, cans, bottle caps, and more. Over time, Bodys' sculptures got bigger and more detailed. He started combining lots of pieces to create massive installations.

ENVISIONING A BETTER FUTURE

Bodys believed that art could change the future, and his extreme maquettes were his vision of new possibilities. His sculptures show cities where people are free and peaceful and work together. Bodys hoped that one day architects would use his cities as inspiration in building a better future.

FAST FACT

He constructed his vision of a better world through maquettes.

Utopian City

Assemble a maquette of a utopian city.

MATERIALS

- Cardboard
- Colored paper
- Recycled materials, e.g., cardboard tubes, plastic packaging, and bottle caps
- Hot glue gun
- Tempera or acrylic paint
- Paintbrushes
- Paint palette
- Water cup
- Scissors
- Mixed media, e.g., sequins, pom poms, chenille stems, and cotton balls

VOCABULARY

MAQUETTE: A planned miniature model of something.

UTOPIA: An ideal community where everything is perfect.

INFRASTRUCTURE: The structures needed to operate a society (e.g., transportation, communication, energy, and water supply).

ART CONNECTIONS

Bodys made miniature models of cities and called them "extreme **maquettes**." These small cities showed his vision of a perfect future for his community, country, and world. He used paper and recycled materials to construct fantastic cities filled with skyscrapers, monuments, stadiums, pavilions, roadways, billboards, and more. His cities were beautiful, and his style was unlike any other. Over time, Bodys' cities got more expansive and became even more detailed. When combined, they would fill entire rooms.

Fig. 1: Assemble and glue your building.

Fig. 2: Paint your building.

Fig. 3: Embellish your building.

122 BE A CREATIVE CHANGEMAKER: A KIDS' ART ACTIVITY BOOK

Let's Get Started!

1: Envision a **utopian** city. This is a community where everything is perfect. Think about the different types of buildings and **infrastructure** you will need to make it an ideal place to live and work.

2: Choose one building to construct first. Use cardboard, paper, and other recycled materials to assemble your building. Use a hot glue gun to attach the pieces. **Fig. 1**

3: Use tempera or acrylic paint to add color to your building. **Fig. 2**

4: Bodys often used small objects and cut paper to cover his buildings in decorative patterns. Once the paint has dried, begin to embellish your building. Consider creating your own patterns using circles, stripes, diamonds, stars, and floral motifs. You can also use mixed-media materials such as sequins, pom poms, chenille stems, cotton balls, and more. **Fig. 3**

5: Follow steps 2 through 4 to construct another building for your utopian city. **Fig. 4**

6: Find a large piece of cardboard to use as the base of your utopian city. Attach both buildings to the cardboard surface. **Fig. 5**

7: Complete your utopian city. Construct additional buildings, roads, monuments, stadiums, parks, and more! **Fig. 6**

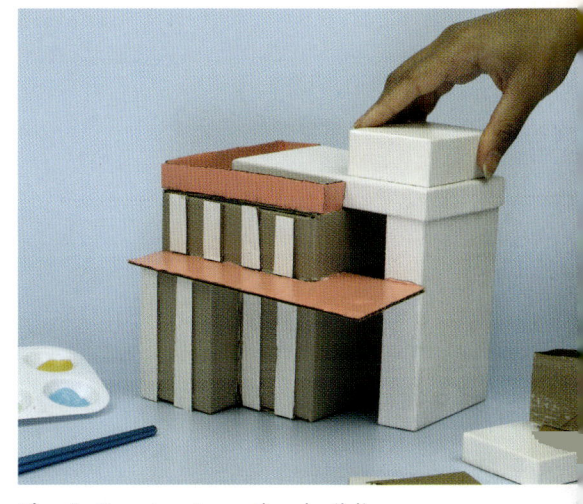

Fig. 4: Construct another building.

Fig. 5: Attach both buildings to cardboard.

Fig. 6: Create more elements to complete your utopian city.

TECHNIQUES & TIPS

- When painting your utopian city, you can use tempera or acrylic paint on paper and cardboard surfaces. However, use acrylic paint if you are painting on plastic or another impermeable surface.

- We all have our vision for a better world, and no single utopia exists for everyone. Create a city that shows your ideas and hope for the future.

About the Author

PAULA LIZ (she/her/ella) is an artist, activist, educator, and author. She was born in Puerto Rico and attended the Maryland Institute College of Art. She has taught art for over a decade in New York, Texas, Washington, DC, and Maryland, where she was named art educator of the year in 2022. The best part of her job is teaching and creating art with kids every day!

Outside the classroom, Paula Liz works to make art education more equitable and inclusive for all. She believes art can change the world and encourages everyone to work together to imagine and create a better future!

Learn more at paulalizart.com.

About the Illustrator

BAMBI RAMSEY is an illustrator, artist, and pattern designer living in Northern California with her family, two dogs, and two rabbits. She works in multimedia, mostly with pen and ink, gouache, watercolor, and graphite, and loves to mix it all together with digital techniques. When Bambi is not drawing, you can find her creating costumes, growing tomatoes, hunting for treasures in antique and thrift stores, or backpacking in the Trinity Alps. Her beautiful daughter Violette is her greatest inspiration.

See more of Bambi's work at bambiramsey.com.

Acknowledgments

Thank you to everyone who made this book possible, especially my family, friends, colleagues, and husband. It is a book I wish I had as a child, and I am honored to have the opportunity to showcase these creative changemakers. I hope the stories and activities here inspire young artists to recognize their creative power and potential!

I also want to express my deep appreciation for the artists featured in this book. Their talents, imagination, and passion pushed boundaries and paved the way for artists worldwide. I also want to thank all the amazing artists who have inspired me and have yet to have their stories told, especially my former and current students. Without you, this book would not have been possible!

Thank you.

References and Resources

Please visit paulalizart.com for references and links to additional resources to expand your creative journey.

Index

A
Abad, Pacita, 117
Aborigines (Australia), 67
Abstract art
    Azurdia, 107
    Escobar, 103
    project, 56–57
    Thomas, 55
Akhenaten (Pharaoh), 11
Amarna (Akhetaten), Egypt, 11
Animal motifs
    painting, 52–53
    Roy, 51
Apartheid, 111
Ashevak, Kenojuak, 95
Azurdia, Margarita, 107

B
Baroque Era, 21
Batik painting
    Kngwarreye, 67
    project, 68–69
Beatty, Talley, 71
Bichos (Clark), 79
Biomorphic forms, 72–73
Burle Marx, Roberto, 79
Bust sculpture
    making commemorative, 12–16
    of Nefertiti, 11
    Thutmose, 11

C
Calderón, Magdalena Carmen Frida Kahlo, 63
Cao Zhi, 11
Caravaggio, 22
Charles II (king of Spain), 31
Chiaroscuro painting
    Gentileschi, 21
    project, 22–23
Chinese art, 17
Circles in My Mind (Abad), 117
Clark, Lygia, 79
Collages
    Azurdia, 107
    community, project, 100–101
    geometric culture, project, 108–109
    Karuga, 99
Colophons, 11
Corot, Jean-Baptiste-Camille, 41
Costume designing, 45–49

D
Degas, Edgar, 41
Drypoint self-portrait project, 26–29

E
Egyptian art, 11
En plein air landscapes, 41–43
The Enchanted Owl (Ashevak), 95
Engraving
    self-portrait project, 26–29
    van Schurman, 25
Escobar, Marisol, 103

F
Ferreira Salgado, Zélia, 79
First Nations (Australia), 67

G
Gaudi, Antoni, 72
Gentileschi, Artemisia, 21
Goncharova, Natalia Sergeevna, 45
Great Wave off Kanagawa (Hokusai), 37
Gu Kaizhi, 17

H
Handscrolls
    Gu Kaizhi, 17
    Nymph of the Luo River, 17
    project, 18–19
Haystacks (Monet), 38
Heartaches (Shahroudy Farmanfarmaian), 83
Hepworth, Barbara, 59
History of art, 8
Hokusai, Katsushika (Tokitarō, Shunrō), 37
Homage to Guatemala (Azurdia), 107

I
Illuminations (Azurdia), 107
Impressionism art movement, 41
Intaglio, 26
Interactive sculpture
    Clark, 79
    project, 80–81

J

Jewelry
- Smith, 71
- using biomorphic forms to make, 72–73

K

Kahlo, Frida, 63
Kakejiku, 18
Kalighat paintings, 51
Karuga, Rosemary, 99
Kingelez, Bodys Isek, 121
Kngwarreye, Emily Kame, 67
Kwali, Ladi, 89

L

La Casa Azul, 63
La Roldana, 31
Landscapes
- en plein air project, 42–43
- making series of drawings of changing, 38–39

Larionov, Mikhail, 45
Last Necklace (Smith), 71
The Learned Maid (van Schurman), 25
Leonardo da Vinci, 22
Lins, Lygia Pimentel, 79

M

Manet, Édouard, 41
Manet, Eugène, 41
Maquettes
- Kingelez, 121
- utopian city project, 122–123

Mirror mosaic, 83–87
Modern art
- Clark, 79
- Escobar, 103
- Hepworth, 59
- Selim, 75
- Smith, 71

Monet, Claude, 38, 41
Monotype printmaking, 83
Monument of Freedom (Selim), 75
Morisot, Berthe, 41
Morisot, Edma, 41
Muafangejo, John Ndevasia, 111

N

Navarro de los Arcos, Luis Antonio, 31
Nefertiti, 11
Nicholson, Ben, 59
Nymph of the Luo River (Gu Kaizhi and Cao Zhi), 11

O

Ōi, Katsushika, 37
One Hundred Views of Mount Fuji (Hokusai), 37, 38
"Organic line," 79

P

"Participatory propositions," 79
Pissarro, Camille, 41
Pottery
- Kwali, 89
- sgraffito vase project, 90–93

Printmaking
- animal prints project, 96–97
- Ashevak, 95
- changing landscapes project, 38–39
- drypoint self-portrait project, 26–29
- Hokusai, 37
- monotype, 83
- Muafangejo, 111
- personal narratives project, 112–113
- van Schurman, 25
- woodblock, 37

Projects
- abstract art, 56–57
- animal motifs, 52–53
- animal prints, 96–97
- assemblage portrait sculpture, 104–105
- batik painting, 68–69
- bust sculpture, 12–16
- changing landscape series, 38–39
- chiaroscuro painting, 22–23
- community collage, 100–101
- costume-making, 46–49
- drypoint self-portrait (printmaking), 26–29
- en plein air landscapes, 42–43
- geometric culture collage, 108–109
- historical figure sculpture, 32–35
- interactive sculpture, 80–81
- mirror mosaic, 84–87
- necklace, 72–73
- painting capturing community, 76–77
- personal narrative prints, 112–113
- scroll painting, 18–19
- sgraffito pottery, 90–93
- subtractive sculpture, 60–61
- symbolic self-portrait, 64–65
- trapunto quilt painting, 118–119
- utopian city maquette, 122–123

R

Relief printing, 96
Renoir, Pierre-Auguste, 41
Retrospectives, 55
Rivera, Diego, 63
Roldán, Luisa Ignacia, 31
Roy, Jamini, 51
Russian folk art, 45

S

Sagrada Familia church (Gaudi), 72
Scroll painting
- Gu Kaizhi, 17
- project, 18–19

Sculpture
- abstract, 59
- assemblage portrait project, 104–105
- Azurdia, 107
- bust project, 12–16
- Clark, 79
- Hepworth, 59
- historical figure project, 32–35
- interactive, project, 80–81
- Kingelez, 121
- La Roldana, 31
- Shahroudy Farmanfarmaian, 83
- subtractive project, 60–61
- Thutmose, 11

Self-portraits
- drypoint project, 26–29
- Kahlo, 63
- symbolic, project, 64–65

Selim, Jewad, 75
Sgraffito pottery project, 90–93
Shahroudy Farmanfarmaian, Monir, 83
Shunrō, 37
Smith, Arthur George, 71

T

Thomas, Alma, 55
Thutmose, 11
Tokitarō, 37
Trapunto quilt painting project, 118–119
Tutankhamun (Pharaoh), 11
Tutuola, Amos, 99

U

Ukiyo-e, 37
Utopian city maquette project, 122–123

V

Van der Passe, Magdalena, 25
Van Gogh, Vincent, 38
Van Schurman, Anna Maria, 25
Venice Biennale, 79

W

Warhol, Andy, 103
Wearable art
- Smith, 71
- using biomorphic forms to make, 72–73

Weir, Barbara, 67
West Baffin Cooperative, 95
Woodblock prints, 37